Marcus Garcia de Almeida

DO YOU THINK I'M STUPID?

A Chronicle of the Corporate World

Find out how complex it can be working in companies with people who think you are...

Ideário

Publication rights reserved to PROFISSIONAIS.COM LTD.

All rights reserved. No part of this book may be reproduced, by any means, especially in photocopy (xerox), without the written permission of Publisher Ideário.

Edition: Marcus Garcia de Almeida

Digital editing, cover and graphic design: IDEÁRIO

Proofreading and English translation:

Marcus Garcia de Almeida Junior e Rodrigo Prata Garcia.

Profissionais.com Ltda.

Rua XV de novembro, 964 – 3º andar – Cj. 30

Bairro Centro – CEP 80060-000 – Curitiba-PR

Phone: (41) 4042-5112

Copyright (c) 2020 by Profissionais.com Ltda.

Official website of the publisher: idearios.com.br

Author's official website: marcusgarcia.com.br

Dados Internacionais de Catalogação na Publicação (CIP)
(Câmara Brasileira do Livro, SP, Brasil)

```
Almeida, Marcus Garcia de
   Do you think I'm stupid? : a chronicle of the
corporate world / Marcus Garcia de Almeida ;
[translation Marcus Garcia de Almeida Junior, Rodrigo
Prata Garcia]. -- Curitiba : Editora Ideário, 2020.

   Título original: Acha que sou idiota? : uma
crônica do mundo corporativo
   ISBN 978-65-991021-2-7

   1. Administração de empresas 2. Cultura
organizacional 3. Governança corporativa
4. Inovações 5. Relações humanas I. Título.

20-46888                                    CDD-658.4
```

Índices para catálogo sistemático:

1. Governança corporativa : Administração de
    empresas   658.4

Cibele Maria Dias – Bibliotecária – CRB-8/9427

Ideário

Summary

Special thanks

For this work I had the support of my family, which is the unconditional basis of everything I do.

I counted on the support of friends who discussed and together we deepened the analysis on the topics covered here. Especially Marcelo, with whom I discussed tirelessly, starting from the book's first sketch to the harshest concepts to make them palatable to everyone.

To the wonderful team of Publisher Ideário, who always surrounded me during the creative journey, never letting me fade down.

To the translators of the work for the English language, Marcus Junior and Rodrigo Prata who were tireless in the intense journey involving this challenge.

Dedication

For Vera.

For all the people who work hard day after day to deliver their best performance in their profession, despite all the hardships they face.

For all entrepreneurs who, because they believe in their idea, decide to take the risks inherent to having their own businesses, being in this way able to make the decisions required and earn the rewards resulting from that, whatever they might be.

For all the professional executives, working in organizations of all types and sizes, who courageously cope with the burden of making the decisions needed to maintain the strategies to which they are subject.

For all workers in organizations of all types and sizes who perform their duties and take part in their responsibilities, believing in their ability to accomplish and fulfill their dreams.

For my father, Lauro (*in memoriam*) and my mother, Eunice, who have been entrepreneurs throughout all their lives, always believing in their potential and never giving up on their dreams.

Preface

Today there's a common understanding that companies have the need to innovate, as they will not be able to keep up with their markets if they don't develop their creative capacity, bringing new solutions and services to customers and getting differentiated, seeking to be a leader in their departments.

Innovation brings forth the possibility to reduce costs and create differentials simultaneously. The point is that these sudden changes do put pressure on executives to quickly change the way they think and seek better understanding of this new world full of inventions and innovations that generate sudden changes in the market.

It's the need to react quickly, as there is neither time nor space to practice a defense, because discontinuity and the phenomenon of disruptive innovation can make markets obsolete overnight.

So what we see is a strong pressure to get ready for all the implications of this innovation universe, which involves working despite the uncertainties, the need to develop genuine and non-programmed creativity in people and especially in tolerating failures, mistakes and errors in projects. These are varied deviations that occur and stress the need to work on speculating futures that will emerge.

The treasure map for those working with innovation has become the search for the Holy Grail, which is creative insight, having the right idea and the opportunity to assess directly with the customer what he wants and expects. It's no longer good enough to use project management methodologies for a perfect implementation of ideas (lower cost, higher quality and lesser risk) in order to get ahead of the competition.

The customer's world requires technological changes and once you have the capacity of having that "Eureka", just put it all together into a new system and then we would have a new process and a magical solution. But this is not how it happens.

One of the most heard mantras in the several competitions in startups and hackathons is "...having an idea is easy, the hard part is to execute it...", having that said, innovation could become more like a game of appearances, rather than actually disposing of the true potential related to the ability of creating brand new realities, more vibrant and more interesting.

At the end of the day, the feeling we have, quite frankly, is that innovation is more of an organizational routine, yet another meeting among the countless meetings we have to attend. It is more an agenda for which we must seek some kind of social representation among other people. The difference is that now we have a budget for that, stick notes, colored pens and blank boards to paint; but this future, which we feel deep down that will never come true, translates into the fear that another organizational routine will be banalized like so many others, making people stop dedicating themselves completely to creative movements that could happen in a very genuine way. It all starts to revolve around the discussion of methods and processes once again and not the matter of the human dimension. We seek the insight, we seek the idea, we seek to stimulate creativity, but nobody wants to live their creative reality...

And then if all this artificial effort is needed, that's because we are fighting against something and the suitable question is: what's holding us back so much?

The creative insight happens suddenly and unexpectedly, creative ones say. It springs from the individual into the world and it's enclosed between the real material world and the abstract world. As it happens in a sudden and unexpected way, it's beautifully and totally unpredictable.

Marcelo Alessandro Fernandes

Part 1

Chapter 1 - Breaking the routine?

Have you noticed that within companies some flagrant situations happen, but managers across many levels just pretend that everything is normal? A co-worker with much less time employed than you gets promoted, and you remain the same. Is it normal? Your boss hires a person much younger than you for a position equal to yours, but earning much less, and the boss leaves you responsible for training the new colleague, because you are quite experienced. Is it normal? You receive an invitation to take on the challenge of a very complex new project because of your vast experience, but your salary does not change. Is it normal?

A coworker in the same department as yours, a big friend of the boss, is able to take a vacation when they want, but your vacation time is allowed only when your boss thinks it's best. Is it normal? You ask your boss to pay at least half of a new course because you are going to take on that very important project, but you are informed that it will not be possible because of the company's cost reduction efforts. Suddenly the company decides to renovate the furniture of all the meeting rooms and spends the biggest money. Is it normal? You ask to switch shifts for two weeks to be able to solve a private issue, but it's not possible due to the reduction of personnel. The following week, your coworker has their shift moved to take care of some private matters. Is it normal? When you return from a business trip, your flight is delayed, so you have to eat dinner at the airport, and it doesn't come cheap. In the expense report of your trip, the company denies the reimbursement for your dinner at the airport because that expense was not foreseen. Is it normal? Your company holds a business dinner to a large customer to seal an important business deal. Even though you were responsible for all the negotiation, managed the relationship and took care of all the details directly with the customer, you are not invited, but your Manager, the Product Manager, the Account Manager and the other specialists, who barely interacted directly with the customer, are invited. Is it normal? Your Manager makes all routes for technical visits to customers, but your route is always the one that goes through the country and small cities, with limited access and lodging in economy hotels. Customers who are in state capitals and major cities, all with air conditioning and lodging in excellent hotels never come to you. Is it normal? Laptops for employee use are being upgraded, but a new computer never comes to you, just refurbished or used ones from other employees. Is it normal?

It's... all normal! Do you think I'm stupid?

One of the things that can be hated the most in day-to-day work are the events and situations with no practical sense that are repeated, that is, they are only there to satisfy a rule or, as they say, to create a false sense of accomplishment. Even worse are the people who repeat themselves, it seems that they lack imagination. There are also careerists[1] who seek, somehow, to gain an advantage in order to move up the organizational hierarchy, even if stepping over someone. What about those abusive and careless people? They are always devising some way of working less to the detriment of other people's work or merit. I cannot forget some managers who seem to exist only to make their employees' lives a living hell. Oh, and the gossipers[2] on active duty? They keep creating rumors and intrigues just to pass the time or to gain some advantage... Well, there are companies where this list can be quite long!

To illustrate more carefully and based on some facts, I will describe how this tangled web of interests can be visceral[3] and at the same time come completely wrapped and disguised in legitimate intentions and desires. This disguise is invariably very intimate and may require a superior ability to perceive day-to-day organizational situations that go far beyond self-help books or on-call theorists.

It all started on the beautiful Monday of December 16, 2019, very early, in which Leonardo was very excited!

As he drove his SUV[4] on his way to work, he felt his heart flutter at his exacerbated emotion. He was excited, but also a little worried, as there was a latent anxiety[5] that showed on his face. He felt it. The last weekend he spent at home enjoying his hobby also served as a way to build up courage and finally be able to do what he had been thinking for weeks.

Even though he was aware of the metropolis' intense traffic, this was not enough to stop him from thinking about the transformation he was about to cause in his colleagues' daily lives as soon as he put his initiative into practice.

He felt his sweaty hands showing a little nervousness. He knew he needed concentration and calm and tried to ease it by listening to his favorite radio station.

"I know I'm going to do something crazy, but I have made my decision!", he thought in a clear attempt to affirm to himself how his thoughts on the sequence of actions he was about to carry out would have an impact for the entire company.

"I will do it! I'm sure of it! I need to give people a reality check. Either I change the way things are going on at the company or I throw in the towel[6]. This can't go on. I am already fed up of seeing the projects being conducted that way. It has been some time since everything started to be done as if it were a cake recipe. Some of the ingredients change, but the base remains unchanged." Thought Leonardo behind the wheel using his mental metaphors. In fact, using metaphors is one of his devices to explain to his subconscious what he is really thinking.

"Projects cannot be seen as cake recipes and my team's knowledge is not an ingredient!", he pondered in his mind with another metaphor.

Leonardo has an innovative spirit[7] and a great desire to transform. He is a young, 35-year-old, single, very determined, and successful in his career that started at the same company where he now works.

Fifteen years ago, he joined the company's trainee program, in the same year he graduated from college in Marketing and Advertising. At that time, late 1990s, as soon as he started his undergraduate course, then at the age of 18, he was clearly aware that the performance of a marketing professional in a company should go far beyond that stereotype of the professional who wore extravagant, psychedelic and multicolored clothes, and who needed to sell an image of a "cool" person who "thought outside the box" with the ability to always bring the unusual and thus help to leverage a company's business through mind-boggling, millionaire campaigns.

Everyone laughed at him and said that he was outdated, that the future would be to increasingly enhance that performance format and that companies would always continue to demand this professional profile. They were wrong, Leonardo was right!

Something that has always bothered Leonardo is the fact that the company he works for is very conservative. He has fought many battles to defend his ideas. It was never his style to want to change things just for changing. Just to break the routine[8]. For him, it is necessary that a change is meant to improve and evolve, preferably breaking with the concepts in force until then. After all, it was like that with Uber, Airbnb, WhatsApp, Facebook, SpaceX, Bitcoin, Ant Financial, Infor and so many others that simply broke with the old way and brought an improved and disruptive way of doing something that was known.

He was not at all happy to see himself and his colleagues as parts of a large arrangement of highly efficient and effective gears[9]. The ability to produce something really new, that could bring a new spirit to themselves, to the company as a whole and of course, to customers, needed to be restored. But in order to turn this great logic into his own corporate microverse he needs to start with the engine of it all: people.

He believes that work, products, services and everything that a team is dedicated to in a company can and should evolve, because he always thought that "... it is part of human nature[10] to evolve and rediscover...", and did not think that this should be different with the people themselves and their ways of working as professionals.

"You can't be stagnant[11]!" Shouted Leonardo in his restless mind. "We need to wake up to the possibilities!", He shuddered in his thoughts.

There was one more challenge that he needed to overcome. Leonardo saw his Director, Teressa, with inconsistent behavior. At the same time that she expressed joy for some results achieved by the company as a whole, she repeatedly said that the company was always at the financial limit and that there were challenges to maintain the execution of the budget plan.

"Gentlemen, the situation requires more austerity! We need to maximize the use of our resources, all of them. We need to reduce costs, all of them. We need to improve operational effectiveness and efficiency in all departments. We are going to make the cycle of continuous improvement[12] work.",

He recalled the cries of his Director, which sounded like a mantra in all meetings with management.

Something that also bothered Leonardo was the fact that Teressa's clear incoherent behavior created a climate that was sometimes hostile. She was harsh with managers, as if they were solely responsible for providing all the answers the company needed in order to improve. By always acting this way, it was common to witness awkward situations in meetings. A bad tension, totally unnecessarily.

"What we need is to create a good tension, that is, one that makes people overcome themselves because they understand that it is possible to do things differently, but also with more satisfaction and better results for everyone. It is not a mere process improvement[13], as if it were calibrating, lubricating and giving preventive maintenance to a machine to produce more and better.", reflected Leonardo, embittered by these essentially utilitarian questions[14]. He realized that there was a bias towards what was considered morally correct. For the Director, it was enough that the decisions and actions produced the greatest positive balance of satisfaction or well-being for all those affected by the action, however in an egotistical[15] way, without considering the interrelations permeating all those involved, that is, employees, customers, suppliers, society, shareholders... Leonardo understood that it would not be enough for each individual to be well, if the group was not well.

His intention arriving at the company that Monday was "...to put a lot of crazy ideas into practice!", which is how he considered them. In fact, it was much more how he thought people would see his idea, because it wasn't just unusual, but also challenging.

He really had his head going and a lot of desire to change that routine and to transform people's mindsets. He also knew that he might not really transform some ways of thinking, at least not at first, but he was sure it would show a new perspective. This alone would allow his colleagues to see that there are more paths, in addition to giving them the opportunity to perceive themselves and thus open up to an internal transformation, one of those that are true and consistent.

"I believe that everyone can rediscover themselves and make a new interpretation of their own professional performance. I understand that this is true happiness!", that was Leonardo's understanding of what a professional should have in their heart.

"The discovery of yourself! That's what I want my colleagues to find! That they can be happy at work, regardless of matters such as salary, organizational climate or personal satisfaction... they will be happy simply because they will help other people with the work that they do... ", Leonardo thought in relation to the theme.

"I understand that salary, organizational climate and personal satisfaction are very important, but they are too basic issues to be taken as determinants of the happiness of a professional, because before we are professionals, we are all people.", considered Leonardo in his mind.

"True happiness must go far beyond these utilitarian issues," reflected Leonardo, with anguish in his chest.

The way Leonardo has always thought of the problems that come to his restless mind is a little unusual. He has a tendency to see and analyze situations holistically[16]. What, according to most people, can be quite complicated, for him it is just a set of elements that are related, interconnected, equalized, transformed and thus solved. Perhaps because he can look further than the vast majority.

Especially this Monday, his mind was certainly not an example of concern, if the things he had thought of doing would cause an effect of strangeness, surprise, disgust, insecurity, fear or denial to his colleagues. What he was sure of was that it would be a shock to the way of looking at work and that would certainly reflect on the company as a whole.

What he also thought about was how it could make him and his colleagues happier, making everyone look far beyond the traditional cake recipe. This is how Leonardo defined the company's way to operate and how he could deliver value to the business which he has already dedicated fifteen years of his work.

"It is true! I am still not one hundred percent sure that what I am about to do will be well accepted. I just know that I need to do it. The work routine is consuming me and making me unproductive. I'm very close to going into my General Director Teressa's office and throw everything up in the air.", he recalled with a warm face.

"I like my job, but the routine is too excruciating. I feel as if I were a remote-controlled automaton and sometimes even like some sort of automated sign spinner who moves around their arms and body and varies the movements depending on the situation.", reasoned Leonardo in his metaphors.

He felt very bad for not having been able to change all that so far, despite many attempts and several strategies he created. This frustration was a much deeper feeling for him, it caused him great anguish, but it was not enough to make him give up, on the contrary, it boosted him more.

In Leonardo's view, his Director is a professional who has a type of coherence and behavior that orbit between 'too resistant to be in an executive position moved by the challenges of permanent change required by the 21st century' and 'Wants to demonstrate a startupper[17] vision that is a little false and unconvincing, reaching the point of ridicule in some situations'.

He finds her resistant in the sense that she doesn't make use of some basic technologies to support the increase in personal productivity, for example, she only takes notes in a paper agenda; she insists on holding meetings with the presence of people on the premises, despite having teleconference structure and video systems available. She also has difficulty in being objective for some agendas, which makes the meetings take much longer than needed to deal with simple matters. And of course, she keeps complaining all the time, putting down people's morale and spirits, leaving them worried and insecure.

On the other hand, he considers her a false startupper, since she's taken the decision to include in the company's furniture and decoration some elements that don't match the current structure and functioning. Leonardo understands that changes in this aspect could be promoted, but the fact is those measures were completely disconnected acts, with no reference, no context and no objective; in other words, totally empty. She had a snooker table placed right in the middle of the meeting room. She arranged for two ping pong tables to be placed in the cafe's lobby and, the most unusual, they installed a huge jacuzzi for eight in the social room. It wouldn't be a surprise to place a climbing wall at the office entrance and a bungee jump at the top of the building.

"All of that was certainly excitement because of the trips she made to some startup trade shows in the United States in early 2019.", he thought.

In fact, this was one of the reasons that led Leonardo to think about his idea and ask himself: to whom he had done all this for and with all this excitement in promoting some shock in the organizational culture, my idea will be wonderful, so, why not?

Among his ideas to improve the ambiance and routine at work, Leonardo thought of taking advantage of some of his energy and will to make his colleagues feel happy and relaxed, leaving things lighter and more fun. At least for his concept of fun and lightness.

When Leonardo entered the company parking lot with the seats folded down and his SUV trunk half open with that huge cardboard box tied behind it and fastened by the seat belt, it was already drawing attention.

— Hi, Leonardo. Good morning! What are you up to this time, boss? — asked a colleague.

— What's up? Do you need a little help? — asked another.

— Here you go again with another one of your weirdo things, huh Leonardo! — said a colleague, also Manager in another department.

— Hey! Are we going to have news today, Leonardo? Is it some Christmas decoration? — asked the friend, already celebrating.

That's exactly what you thought! Leonardo had already made some previous attempts to make a change and improve the level of happiness of colleagues in the company, only in more discreet ways that did not involve unusual and unknown things in family-sized cardboard boxes.

It was because of these odd things or inventions, which is how some colleagues call the innovation initiatives presented by him, that the company managed to increase operational efficiency by over ten percent in the last two years, reduce the loss rates in some production lines to less than one percent and create extra services that generated an increase in customer loyalty by more than twenty percent. Metrics that would have never been achieved if things had not changed.

Yes, they are great indicators, but this isn't perceived by Teressa this way, as she believes these achievements are the merit of the company's own organizational structure, of its perfectly aligned processes, of its impeccable quality control and of its highly engaged and qualified teams that enjoy an organizational environment which is incredibly positive.

Naturally, the teams were decisive for these achievements, but before that, there was Leonardo's initiative to propose the transformation, yet initially in a controversial way, to some practices and ways of doing things and that triggered great performance indicators.

— Good morning, Leonardo! What's in the box? It looks heavy! — Lucy asked with some curiosity.

His Personal Assistant, who has her desk by the window, noticed the movement in the parking lot around Leonardo's SUV and went down to the parking lot to help in whatever way she could. Lucy is very proactive.

— No need to worry, Lucy. The box is more bulky than heavy! — he replied, grateful for her willingness to help.

Lucy, Leonardo's personal assistant is a wonderful person and a very competent professional. He hired her about two years ago. At first, his intention was to have a dedicated secretary. Over the initial months, however, Lucy demonstrated a differentiated skill in staying impartial over practically everything at work and still managed to be impartial to interpersonal issues and difficulties. This was decisive for him to decide to have her closer, in a more complex role, as his personal assistant. Then, he authorized her to hire a secretary herself to take care of the agenda and other administrative and operational issues.

— Would you like me to see if your Director's schedule this morning is available? Have you talked to her about this? Since you didn't ask me for anything, I didn't book any time.

She worries about not letting Leonardo expose himself. He is bringing news without telling Teressa in advance. Whenever this happens, he is sometimes euphoric, when his ideas are well received, but gets unbearably moody when receiving a negative.

Yes, you got it right again! Leonardo had already taken some actions in the absence of his Director, which created some stress, much more in her than in him, because Leonardo is unpredictable and despite not being easily overwhelmed, he changes his mood too much.

— It's not necessary, Lucy. I can handle this and talk straight to her. Anyway, thanks for worrying and for the support. — Leonardo said it gratefully.

Lucy was watching the going-on there. Leonardo organized the withdrawal of the box, releasing the restraints and coordinating the help he received from two more colleagues to transport the box up, on the eighth floor, where the Marketing and Products department is and which he is the Manager of.

— Do you want me to carry something for you? After all, I'm already here, let me help you. — Lucy said that being very willing.

He looked at her and thought for a couple of seconds what else he couldn't forget to take upstairs and remembered a little box on the front seat. "Too important!", he thought.

— Right! Please, take that tiny box on the front seat and bring it for me! — Leonardo asked her calmly.

There already were a good number of people around Leonardo's SUV, about 30 people, and some others were gathering quickly.

— Attention, folks! Take it easy! You will soon figure it out. For now, all that I can say is that we're causing a big stir in all the company. Now, please, let's get into the office! — Leonardo said it, showing a large conviction of himself.

The people in the crowd dispersed and headed to their offices. Lucy and two other colleagues remained with Leonardo, helping him to carry the box. As he said, it was huge, but very light. It didn't weigh more than 15 pounds, but at least three people were needed to carry it safely.

The company where Leonardo works is located in its own building in a neighborhood where important national and multinational companies are concentrated. The headquarter is new and very well cared for. This is revealed in the details. In the lobby, the access to the building environment is very organized and of extreme taste and beauty. Everything had been thought out to convey a sense of balance and sobriety, but at the same time managing to maintain a contemporary style. A few asymmetrical trimmings with moderate curves and neutral colours occupy the sideboard next to the waiting area. Minimalist in some details, as in decoration and ornaments, but ostentatious[18] in others, as the company's logo forged in brushed steel supported on a white marble pedestal. Very impressive, at first sight!

The smell of cleanliness is fragrant and creates a sense of peace and tranquility that hangs in the air. The colors are sober, well-balanced, and the natural lighting that enters through the huge glazed facade, whose ceiling reaches 16 feet high in the lobby, highlights the discreet adornments. All this is permanently surrounded by a soft fragrance that resembles something between roses and lavender. A delight, able to make the ones who arrive there feel calm and welcome.

The receptionist on the shift is friendly, very attentive and welcomes Leonardo and his helpers with a wide smile on her face and a pleasant and resounding good morning! Leonardo likes her very much, professionally speaking. In his opinion she is the best among the three receptionists. The most authentic. "Such a sweetheart!" he always says when referring to her.

Leonardo and his helpers went to the service elevator. The box required the larger elevator. Through it, he would arrive at his department with calm and reservation, without the risk of causing troubles in the main elevator. Only Leonardo and the box followed in the service elevator, because it would not fit them all, the others took the main elevator.

— Eighth Floor! — it's announced by a soft digital voice.

The colleagues that were already there helped Leonardo to take out the box and put it in the middle of the room close to Leonardo's office. The other colleagues did not save comments and a buzz quickly settled there. People's curiosity was already stimulated. Without worrying too much, Leonardo greeted everyone with his traditional "good morning, good morning, good morning", left the box there and took the main elevator going straight to the Board of Director floor.

The entire company building is automated and fits into this new generation of smart and sustainable buildings. Special glass facades that let light through, but block the heat; smart taps in the toilets and bathrooms; usage of rainwater in the toilets; elevators with electric regeneration system; air conditioning system with individual and automated temperature control; biometric access control in the areas designated as security sensitive; double discharge toilets for liquid and solid waste; several advancements in access security; increased physical and logical building safety; advanced detection, prevention and combat of smoke and fire outbreaks; harnessing of energy throughout the structure and much more.

Leonardo was the great supporter for the company to move into this new building, as headquarters, in which he demonstrated that after five years it would start to generate savings to pay off its own costs and that all investment needed to change the company's headquarters would fully return in ten years and would generate in the following years savings of at least twenty-two percent per year. In addition, the panoramic view of the neighborhood and the city is wonderful.

The sun was already high around 9:30 am.

— 20th floor! — the usual soft voice announces in the elevator.

Leonardo knew that he should have talked to Teressa about his intention beforehand and only acted afterwards, but he was taken by the excitement he was over the weekend, when he was sure he was making the right decision with his initiative, he ended up messing up things. Not to mention, when it comes to Leonardo, that was nothing new!

"Leonardo is really very sure of himself and his ability. I've never seen any manager doing what he does, in the way he does and being always very respected and assertive!", Lucy thought, who was watching Leonardo a little concerned this morning.

"So, I'm here... not afraid to be happy; come on!" Leonardo thought, trying to tone down some of his insecurity in a mental gesture of self-assertion!

Teressa never denied Leonardo an appointment, even without prescheduled time. Whenever he looked for her there was a good reason for that, at least from his perspective of what could be considered a good reason at the level of a Chief Executive Officer, who has the responsibility to direct and maintain balance and financial health, the investments in product development and business performance as a whole.

The issue is that considering he never received a denial in this way, it made him think that he had the most consistent criteria with total sense for his General Director. This left him reckless and exposed to the protocols of the company hierarchy. It is not uncommon, for example, for him to appear in the middle of a Board meeting and bring up issues that should be dealt with by his General Director. But that's how he has been successful in his initiatives at the company.

— Miss Stella! Good Morning! Please, can you announce I'm here to Teressa? I need five minutes with her! — Leonardo spoke to the Executive Assistant, a mature and highly respected person throughout the company.

According to Leonardo's assessment, Miss Stella is an incredible person. She is extremely cultured. She loves reading the classics of literature and is always very up to date with everything that's happening: general news, those inherent to business and the financial market. She is also totally tuned in to what circulates on social networks in general, with special attention to the company's employees who work at the strategic tactical level[19].

Miss Stella has worked with Teressa for almost twenty years. She has an extensive and solid academic background. Her knowledge goes beyond the general scope, reaching out to the company's business. She is always concerned with studying, improving and reading. She could belong to any position in the company, but her desire was always to be assisting the General Director, taking part in the discussions and executive questions that arise. Her role is that of Executive Assistant and she's always present in the decision-making process. Teressa fully relies on Miss Stella's fair judgment to support her decisions.

— Hey, Leonardo! Yes of course! Just a minute, please ... she'll see you in a few minutes! — Miss Stella said, always very cordial and kind.

— Leonardo, in the meantime while Teressa doesn't call you yet! What news are you bringing along now? Something I should be concerned about as Executive Assistant? — Miss Stella asked, knowing that Leonardo tends to bring somewhat random and odd surprises which could potentially cause disorder, inconvenience or both.

— No, Miss Stella. It's all right! There's nothing to worry about. I'm just bringing a new element to boost the creativity of the staff. It will be very nice... — Leonardo replied, failing to convince the cunning Miss Stella.

— Still, you seem a little agitated, Leonardo. I can notice some anxiety. Wouldn't you be up to something very unusual, my dear colleague? — Miss Stella insisted, due to Leonardo's reputation for his occasional extravagant actions.

— Miss Stella, let me ask you. Said Leonardo, responding to her insistence. — How do you like the fact that we're here in this wonderful new headquarters, saving a lot of money for the company, while bringing much more comfort and quality of life for us all? How do you like the results we have achieved in recent years, always growing? How do you like our level of operational efficiency? — Leonardo went on, speaking in a reserved, but firm voice!

— Yes, Leonardo. We enjoy all of that! — Miss Stella replied, calmly.

— Okay, and you know that all this was only possible due to my firm performance, although sometimes a bit misunderstood, proposing and implementing changes, whereas everyone saw problems and obstacles, don't you? — Leonardo continued, imposing himself gently.

— Of course, I know. Your ideas and attitudes towards some changes were critical in making all this possible. — Miss Stella affirmed.

— Then, my dear colleague. Rest assured! Everything will be fine... — Leonardo was speaking, when Teressa went out the door, waving her hand so that he could enter her office.

— Hi, Leonardo! — Teressa greeted him. — Please come in! — she invited. — Miss Stella told me you wanted to talk quickly. Go ahead! — she said.

— Good morning! How are you doing? — Leonardo says hi with enthusiasm, joy and a smile on his face, trying to hold back his anxiety about what could be on the way.

He knows that previously, his breakthroughs and achievements were positive for the company and that he has recognition from all colleagues for this, including the Board of Directors as a whole and even the Executive Office, especially Teressa. Nevertheless, he was afraid not to be understood this time. At least not immediately.

As he spoke and showcased his idea, providing many good arguments, making the appropriate justifications and listing the pros that the company as a whole could have with his new initiative, Leonardo started to feel a little insecure and the General Director's office seemed to become suffocating in the face of the sheer fury that was building up right in front of him. It appeared at one point that she was about to grab his neck and squeeze it. Her face turned red and the look in her eyes was nothing friendly. They were dull and serious. They were borderline threatening.

— NO, Leonardo ... no way! Did you lose your mind for good? You can stop it and take it all away! We can't bring these things here to the office. It will be a huge distraction all the time and for everybody! — Teressa said, shouting. — And besides, why didn't you discuss this with me before? Why bother to call? You have my direct number and you know you can call me anytime.

— But you haven't even seen it yet! It's going to be great, fun, stimulating and safe. For everybody. I'm sure everyone will love it! We need the staff's imagination to be on the top... we need to advance to a new level, as we are stagnant in this regard. Or haven't you noticed yet? — Leonardo justified, presenting the technical arguments.

— For the last time, Leonardo, the answer is NO! And stop talking nonsense. We are not stagnant! We are very well! Your department is great! You can't keep saying that. It doesn't help at all, you know? We have grown by more than ten percent a year for the past three years! We have enough worries already to deal with before having another of your crazy things around here. — The General Director spoke, quite loudly.

— But ... I just managed to finish with this idea last night, there was no time to talk to you ... I needed ... — Leonardo tried to resume, when he was harshly interrupted.

— ENOUGH! The answer is NO... — Teressa concluded. — Now please will you excuse me; I have a busy schedule ahead of me. Monday has just started, and I have a lot to do. — she asked Leonardo to leave.

The General Director's cries echoed across the 20th floor. It was a hard blow for Leonardo, even if he knew about Teressa's momentum, that response and the way it happened were disconcerting. He had received negatives before, but not in such a hard, definitive way.

Even after being confronted with such harshness, wild look in her look, expression and even intentions, as it seemed at a certain point that Leonardo was going to get physically hit, even so, he kindly thanked her, turned his back and left the room calmly, with all elegance and while leaving, Leonardo thought.

"That's right! I know, I know, I know ... I really should have talked to her; discussed it beforehand! I might as well have called her last night. Now I will have to take away everything that I brought with such care and affection. On top of that, will I be given the label of, who knows, that I lost the temper with my own General Director?", Leonardo thought as he left the room.

The people in the lobby, waiting to be received by the General Director were looking at Leonardo with a mix of pity, awe and fear as he passed by with his best look of pride and tranquility, greeting people and faking a lot of smiles.

— It seems like things didn't go as you planned, right Leonardo? — Asked Miss Stella, in a calm and conciliatory tone. — May I do something? If you give me more details, perhaps I could help! — She insisted.

— No, Miss Stella. Thank you! I'm going to gather my pieces; find the dignity I have left and try to get my head together. I really appreciate it, but we'll talk later. — Leonardo said goodbye, very upset.

— All right, Leonardo. Just, please, do not perform any more deeds for today, agreed? — Miss Stella advised.

Chapter 2 - The deed

What was on Leonardo's mind?

In a way, at the time of the events, nothing was very well structured yet. All the things he sensed were drawing and forming little by little in his mind. A complex process! It seemed that his deepest desires to try to make people gradually assimilate a transformation to a freer and lighter organizational culture, to have a more open form of organizational functioning, were being rejected, destroyed, hated, slaughtered and buried. "How sad!", he thought.

Judging by Teressa's attitudes, in practice, Leonardo's reading was that, in fact, there was a latent feeling within her that it was necessary to recreate the organization's way of being and functioning, but it was clear that she did not know how to do this, or even where to start. It seemed that a certain fear of taking this leap of faith[20] had settled in her.

"What would Teressa's intention be, for example, with a pool table in the meeting room, ping pong tables in the coffee area, and a giant hot tub in the middle of the 'events' room? It could not have been just a Dantesque[21] response to the startup fads", thought Leonardo. "Something is pressing my General Director's head to transform the company, but she is lost in her actions!", concluded Leonardo.

And he did not think of Dantesque with malice, but with the sense of being a merely utilitarian initiative. This was Leonardo's thinking about Teressa's tough position.

He knew and felt it was as if she said that she needed to recreate the company's way of being and existing, but she did not believe enough in the capacity and potential of the people who are there. By his reading, it ended up generating a kind of paradox within the organizational structure, that is, she knew of the need to innovate to make this organizational structure survive, but for that it would be necessary to modify the way the business structure itself works, which would only be achieved with a new way of thinking about how the company works, that is, innovating.

"That's it!", he thought. This thought seems to have brought a new enthusiasm to Leonardo.

He still had an important asset up his sleeve, because until that moment nobody had met Filomena yet. He just commented on it with Lucy and Teressa, but he hadn't introduced her to anyone yet.

"That's it! When they see her, when they finally meet Filomena, I'm sure they'll fall in love! It will be a way to break this paradox of innovation", thought

Leonardo, renewing his hope of advancing his plans, even if Teressa was absent, once again.

— Eighth floor! — Leonardo kept listening to that soft digital voice, thinking what it would be like if the building had elevator operators.

"It would be really cool!", he thought.

"I would certainly discuss the general impressions of everything I had heard while transporting people all day up and down between the 25 floors of our company's headquarters building." But all he had was that velvety, smooth digital voice.

"Patience! We can't have everything we want!", Leonardo agreed.

Leonardo left the elevator elegantly and with a completely renewed spirit and went to his office, asking Lucy to accompany him. He was not going to give up: he would not throw in the towel and neither would he kick the bucket, even after receiving that direct order from his General Director to take everything away. The main fact that encouraged him was that she, the General Director, had not told him that he had to comply immediately, so he thought: "Get to work...".

— How was it with the General Director, Leonardo? Were you able to talk about your initiative? Did everything work? — asked curiously, Lucy.

— I did talk to her, yes, but the result was not promising. She said to take everything away, that I can't go on with my initiative, that I'm crazy... these things. I got really upset. But what I think really happened is that she was much more disappointed in the fact that I didn't speak to her in advance, rather than not approving my proposal. — considered Leonardo.

— Well, Leonardo. You know very well that there is always a very fine line that separates logic and corporate trickery, on opposite sides of very different trenches. Did she explicitly tell you to take everything away immediately?

Leonardo's eyes lit up when he heard his Personal Assistant ask him what he himself had already considered moments before. It looked like a warning, a green light. He looks at her steadily and says that he has not been given an order to act immediately.

— In fact, Lucy, she was inaccurate in her words. In reality, she was mad at me for going over her with my initiative and having already brought everything here... without talking to her in advance, you know?

— Well, then, in that case, I think you should get down to business and continue whatever you thought about Filomena here in the office. — encouraged Lucy.

— And speaking of Filomena, when will I meet her? Asked Lucy.

— Have a little more patience, Lucy. Soon, you, the whole company... everyone will meet her!

Leonardo was now moving to the other side of the trench and knew the risks that this would pose for him, for his colleagues and probably for the company's image if the whole thing, by some chance of fate, got out of control. He decided to risk it all!

Definitely "... take it all back home!", was not a priority for Leonardo. On the contrary, he decided that he would go ahead. He asked for help from some colleagues, who, despite not understanding his intentions with that whole equipment, helped. Something Leonardo wasn't sure about, and the reason he was still a little uncomfortable, is if his colleagues were helping him just because he is the boss or if it was because they were really curious to see what was going to happen.

"Ah, what the hell! You can't wish to be sure of everything and to want to understand what goes on in everyone's mind when it comes to transforming people. I really have to face the situation and go ahead! I need to believe in my instincts!", Leonardo was convinced, reaffirming to himself the intention of achieving his intent, even if taking risks and exposing his colleagues and the company as a whole.

The box was large due to the contents being fragile and requiring several layers of internal protection. There were styrofoam protectors, bubble wrap, cardboard supports, bags of air, packing peanuts, and cardboard protectors that were being removed part by part. Very carefully, the puzzle was being revealed. Leonardo opened the big box and unpacked and organized everything so he could show everyone what he brought.

But the business environment is a box full of surprises. It does not matter what position you hold or your status with colleagues. Yes! You can be sure! There are people who are truly believers of the style of communication that is more proactive than structured, that is, they love to gossip. These people are always on call. They don't waste time! More than quickly the news of Leonardo's deed was already in the ears of Miss Stella, Executive Assistant to the General Director, Teressa, and that certainly at the first opportunity she would fulfill her obligation and duty to bring to her knowledge what she had learned. But like all responsible, ethical, and senior professional, she would not do this without first checking the facts.

— Hello, Lucy! Good morning, how are you? Please, Lucy, how are things there on the eighth floor? Is Leonardo doing something new today? — asked Miss Stella.

— Hi, Stella! Everything right here. Yes, Leonardo is setting up something that he brought earlier today to the office, here in the hall next to his office. — replied Lucy directly.

— And everything is fine? I mean, is it causing any inconvenience?

— Well, Stella, the inconvenience is not being greater than that time when he made the draws to assemble the rafting teams. At least for now, it's all good, although folks are getting very curious! The area here is a little bit messy too, but nothing too serious... soon it's all going to be figured out.

Miss Stella checked with Lucy and despite knowing about her loyalty to Leonardo, she knows about her exemption from the facts. Then she was calm and sure that there was no reason to be alarmed, and now she knows in what tone she should inform Teressa as soon as she has the chance.

Of course, the proactive information keeps coming to Miss Stella. As they are unstructured, as they move from one person to another, they suffer the well-known phenomenon of information noise, that is, events start to arrive like this: "... look, another madness from Mr. Leonardo, Manager here at our department. It is generating one non-conformity after another in relation to safety and the rules for the use of shared office space, imposing some restrictions on the transit of employees through the hallways and other spaces, including affecting the ergonomic risk of the work environment!", and this is a beautiful, elegant, and accurate way to deliver the information. There are people who prefer to communicate that way. Gossip, when transmitted like that, makes it look more believable.

But there are people who, despite participating in the same group of supporters of unstructured proactive communication, do not do so with such beauty, nor with elegance, nor with the accuracy required to avoid distorting or increasing the intensity of the facts. That is, the reports originating from this other group of people were also delivered to Miss Stella, but as "... and now Leonardo has gone mad for good! It's making the biggest mess here on the eighth floor. He's opening a gigantic box, filled with some weird materials here in our work area. He's spreading a lot of things everywhere. This is looking more like a dorm room than an office. Almost a war zone or a scrapyard. A lot of noise, dirt, and a big mess. One can't work like that. This is even unhealthy".

To everyone's surprise, it was taking too long for someone to go there. Perhaps the Facilities Manager, or Human Resources, concerned with OSHA (Occupational Safety and Health Administration) and overall safety of the work environment , to restore normality by ordering the immediate removal and collection of any and all material foreign to the work environment, that was quickly accumulating.

But none of this was on the verge of happening, at least not by the hour, and while none of this was happening, Leonardo, who is very capricious, was unpacking things, calmly, carefully, and lovingly. His concern was that Filomena could have the necessary infrastructure to win over everyone with her charm and grace, reversing all the odds that were against him.

He was really immersed in his task of organizing everything while humming a song he heard on the radio earlier from his favorite band – an explicit declaration of insanity, madness or even subversion.

Leonardo loves it!

Piece by piece... part by part... element by element, Leonardo put everything up: the supports, the trails, the different environments, the passage tubes and paths. The different spaces like the leisure area, the gym patio, the bathroom, the eating area, the bedroom, the balcony, the woods, the ball pit, the dance floor, the automated elevator... all arranged very carefully. "Wow! It's getting beautiful!", he thought. Some people asked, curious, because they still had not been able to understand what he was assembling there or why he was doing it.

Everything was very playful, unusual, colorful, magical and curious. People's imagination was flying high...

— But what is this, Leonardo? What's all this for? Is it some kind of diorama or model for a new product? A toy track? Is it a maze? How interesting! — asked a colleague, in a strange tone.

— Wow! Do you know what this looks like? A maze for a RC car! Cool... my son loves cars. — said another.

— Is it more Christmas decoration for our department, Leonardo? — asked another.

— Leonardo, what are you going to put in there? Is it for some kind of new video game? Can we play too? — asked a colleague, very excited about everything.

— Is it a prototype for any new product, Leonardo? — Asked a colleague.

— Calm down guys, you'll soon understand, okay? Just a little more time and everything will be ready! — said Leonardo, calming the mood of the staff.

In general, everyone was really, really curious.

"How cool, one of my goals already seems to be being achieved!", celebrated Leonardo in his thoughts.

However, there was also already gossip. Some colleagues commented that they were afraid that this attitude of Leonardo could end up harming everyone in the department. "Very daring!", some thought.

On the other hand, it was clear that there were already several colleagues who were anxious and wanted to meet Filomena, even though they still did not know what it was or what it was supposed to be. They couldn't wait, and even started calling her by the name. "When are we going to meet Filomena, Leonardo? Will it take long?" asked some. "Be patient, people. Just a little while longer.", replied Leonardo, patiently.

Some other colleagues, however, despite the natural curiosity, were afraid of the consequences of having the one that Leonardo was setting up right there, in the middle of the room on the eighth floor of the department in which he is Manager. A real foreign body to the company's structure, assembled right there for everyone to see. "Wow, I wish I had

Leonardo's courage!", some thought. "Leonardo is freaking out. What is he trying to prove?", reflected others. "I hope he gets burned this time!", a few wished.

It did not take long, and it was clear that the inevitable ended up happening, after all, we are in the era of digital information and fast, pervasive, and omnipresent communication. Some colleagues that were more excited by all that movement and news of the unusual deed being drawn right in front of them started taking photos. Others started making videos and sharing everything on social media.

Some comments and hashtags were starting to multiply. A true curiosity party in the company's social networks, the corporate intranet:

"Revolution in the office... #MyManagerHasGoneCrazy";

"Manager set up an unusual object right in the middle of the office! #MyManagerHasGoneCrazy #BraveManager";

"The manager went crazy. What would this be? Anyone who might know please tell me in the comments!
#DifferentOffice #BraveManager
#MyManagerHasGoneCrazy";

"Does anyone know what this is in the photo? My manager set up right in the middle of the office.
#DifferentOffice #BraveManager
#MyManagerHasGoneCrazy";

"Has anyone ever heard of a 'Filomena'? Do you know if it's a new toy? #Filomena #BraveManager #NewToy";

"A toy house is set up in the middle of the office. Did the manager go crazy? #Filomena #BraveManager #NewToy";

"Overwork leads manager to assemble a kind of toy in the middle of the company's office! #Filomena #BraveManager #NewToy #Workaholic";

"Here in my department everything happens! There is no monotony! What about yours? #BraveManager #Filomena #NewToy #Workaholic";

"My manager is the GOAT! He's revolutionizing the routine around here in the office! Let's enjoy, comment and share... #Filomena #BraveManager #NewToy #Workaholic";

"The Amazing Filomena! #Filomena #CrazyManager #NewToy #Workaholic #TheAmazingFilomena".

With all the buzz around the office and in the intranet, the result could not be different. Employees from other departments of the company learned about the movements on the eighth floor. Some could not resist their curiosity and went there to see it up close. Others, completely taken by their curiosity, as they could not leave their desks, popped even more messages both on the company's intranet and outside of it, on the Internet. While some people were arriving at the scene, the more daring started broadcasting live.

The power of organic sharing on social media showed its strength and in a few minutes everything that was happening there gained popularity, was widely shared, and hundreds of employees and people from outside the company were watching live the unusual saga in the office, kicked off by Leonardo!

Friends, colleagues, acquaintances, friends of friends, colleagues of colleagues, acquaintances of acquaintances, relatives, business partners, competitors, suppliers, customers... the whole thing got out of control!

Some memes came up and the hashtags #Filomena, #BraveManager, #Workaholic and #MyManagerWentCrazy multiplied.

"Ah, the Internet! The story of my climb towards the transformation of people in the work environment, of my colleagues and of the business environment as a whole is beginning to gain some shape that frightens me a little. I think that all that's missing now is to be on national network through the traditional radio and TV channels as a character in one of those sensationalist headlines about the executive who turns into a joke for trying to transform the people in the workplace, and is thrown in the middle of the street by security personnel of the own company he used to work for.", thought

Leonardo, while fitting the last part of what he was assembling.

Social media is a marvel. It has the power to spread information very quickly. It is fantastic, but also ruthless. What was supposed to be a private initiative by a well-intentioned manager who seeks to improve the creative capacity of his team, soon gains proportions of a small TV variety show.

It didn't take long for Leonardo's mother to call him during office hours, a rare thing to happen, unless she had a health emergency or some other problem. There are mothers who are very proud of their children, and there are those helicopter mothers, who follow their children step by step in everything they do. They are true fans of their own children. Some are all that and still very tech savvy, they follow everything about their children live on social media. Leonardo's mother is of the latter type.

— Leonardo... my son! I just received a lot of messages here on my social media saying that you were going viral on the Internet. I was seeing you on a live right now. Are you getting famous in the company and didn't tell mom? Did you want to surprise me? — she asked on the phone.

— You know what it is, mom? It's a joke by the team here at the office, everything is fine, no reason to worry! — replied Leonardo.

Of course it is not at all easy to convince your own mother that everything is fine, when dozens of people are on the Internet on social media saying that you are having a mental breakdown, saying that you should be fired and suggesting that you should be taken to the doctor.

— But I see some people here calling you... crazy? Revolutionary? Is everything really fine? What are you up to, my son? Tell your mother, tell me! I also read in a post just now, someone talking about Filomena. There is even a #TheAmazingFilomena. Is she fine? Is Filomena okay? Really? What does she have to do with this? Leonardo, did you take Filomena to the office with you today? — asked the mother, already a little nervous.

— Stay calm, mom. Everything's OK! Really! It's just a social experiment that I'm doing. — he said to his mother. — By the end of the day everything will be solved. Stay calm, okay? — Leonardo amended to calm his mother.

— But did you need to involve Filomena in this, son? That's your work environment, son! Are you going to cause trouble... again? Is Filomena with you now? Is everything okay with her? She's not scared, is she? — She asked, now quite distressed with the situation.

— Mother, listen! I already said. Be calm, okay? Filomena is with me, yes! She's fine! And no, she is not scared. And no, I'm not getting into any trouble. Now I need to hang up, okay? — Replied Leonardo. — We'll talk again soon. Kisses, mom! I love you... Bye! — Leonardo said goodbye to his mother, hanging up the phone.

Leonardo's mother was not a fool or anything. She knew that he was, indeed, in trouble. And it was not small. This was very evident on social media and spreading very quickly. She knew she needed to find out more details about what was going on, and the information needed to come from safe and reliable sources. She knows Miss Stella... and was going to call her! Or maybe send a message... "Yes, it's office hours... better to send her an audio message...", thought Leonardo's mother.

"Hello, Stellie, my dear. How are you? This is Karen, Leo's mom. Listen, do you know what my son is doing in the office today that is appearing on the Internet? They are talking about him... Is everything all right?", Leonardo's mother sent the message to Miss Stella.

"Hi, Karen. I'm good. Yes, Leonardo is doing some activities here with his team and they are all very curious. Even I am! But rest assured that everything is fine. If I have news, I'll let you know. Kisses!" Miss Stella replied reassuringly to Leonardo's mother.

Leonardo's mother, Karen, was much more at ease with the information she received from Miss Stella, at least it was information from a person she knew to be reliable.

There is a moment when some decisions are made within us that generate a feeling of power or empowerment, or both. It is as if you are going to enter alone in a dark and unknown cave in a forest far from civilization. There is a mixture of fear, insecurity, the stomach drops, dread... the adrenaline pours through your veins and makes you stay alert and ready to fight, flight, freeze, or defend yourself from whatever may appear... in the darkness. After the initial impact of the transition from light to the dark interior of the cave, as soon as your eyes get used to the darkness; the sound also changes. The sound of the wind rustling the leaves of the trees gives way to silence and the echo of drops that descend from the stalactites and drip creating puddles along the dark path. The crackle of insects and the sound of your own walking as you step on the damp earth, there is the feeling that there is much more there than your senses reveal... and then, at that moment, your imagination begins to fill the information void with thoughts of dangers that may or may not exist, because everything is in your mind. It is at this point that you have two options: to dominate your mind and feel empowered to move into the unknown, or to feel that there is a power beyond you that should not be faced at that moment and then you step back.

Leonardo was on the verge of deciding what to do... thousands of messages swarmed through social media of people connected directly and indirectly to him. All of it put some pressure on him.

The math behind network multiplication is fantastic. Leonardo has connections in his company, directly connected to him, also called 1st degree connections, just over two hundred people. In Leonardo's company, just over five thousand employees work. The question that arises is: how can the contact with two hundred people reach five thousand almost instantly? Simple, if each of the two hundred people who connect with Leonardo, have a connection with just 20 more people in addition to the 200 that Leonardo already has, then a demonstration on his network has the potential to reach over four thousand people instantly. This is considering only the intranet, that is, only the internal environment of the company.

Now imagine the full potential of the Internet... it's like a viral spread; it is no wonder that the term "it went viral" became so popular with the advent of social media.

It was already after 10:30 am and Leonardo's situation was very close to reaching a chaotic stage, maybe even... irreversible... "(...) there will be consequences...", and that was the greatest certainty that he had, but at that moment he just couldn't measure the proportion, the extent, the severity and the consequences of his actions, besides that "...everything was under control!", thought Leonardo, trying to minimize the situation that he himself created.

Nice control!

A deep conviction that organizational culture effectively precedes innovation took over Leonardo's whole being. "If I have to be the martyr of this situation to transform what is set, stagnating me, my colleagues and everyone else, I am willing to do that!", he thought.

The feeling of putting yourself as a martyr to a cause or an idea, can appear as a breakthrough in someone, but also as a response to self-love. By being placed in situations that test your limits of personal pride and even your convictions; it seems that a kind of overwhelming force rises in your chest that you did not know you could have within you. In these situations, the emotional balance is necessary and the support of a close person to it can be decisive, so that the decision is not merely passionate, but keeps coherent to its principles without losing sight of its convictions. Leonardo knew how to do this, despite many of his attitudes always showing otherwise.

"You know what? I'm fine. Really! I've never been so well! After all, I believe not only in the impact of my initiative, which is necessary, but also in the need to demonstrate my point of view to everyone. Either I do it today, or I will feel really bad, with myself, with my colleagues and with my conscience!", reflected Leonardo, reinforcing his intention mentally.

He knows that people in general are very afraid to reveal themselves, to demonstrate and to illustrate what they think and feel. They prefer to keep holding to it, keeping it all to themselves, to the point that they are completely unhappy, withdrawn, closed or all of this together, even getting into depression. And this is not only at work, but in their lives in general: in the family, at school, in society... "But what a crazy thing!", he thought. "This is a waste! I cannot continue to live with the situation and leave my colleagues in the same fate!", Leonardo demanded of himself.

It seems that people face some insurmountable barriers to a type of social morality that Leonardo doesn't quite understand how it works. It is as if everyone is in a minefield with traps scattered along the path of the most legitimate demonstrations and ideas. This feeling of fear ends up suppressing the way of thinking and understanding the world and is pressing hard for you to swallow your own opinions and ways of thinking, otherwise they will blow you up at any moment.

"Well, I'm fine, I'm confident that everything will be resolved and, even better, I know that the curiosity of the colleagues is already a good indication that I'm probably on the right path.", thought Leonardo, reclusive in his thoughts and determined to proceed.

After finishing tidying up and assembling everything that was in the big box, fitting several pieces and connecting several transparent and colored tubes, it was finally ready!

"Now is the time to charm people," thought Leonardo. "It is time for everyone to meet Filomena.", he concludes in his mind.

Chapter 3 - Setting up the stage

Leonardo is fascinated by the simple things.

He's a very imaginative person.

Whenever our imagination receives a stimulus and this happens in a primordial way, that is, using mainly oral narrative, the archetypes that are in the unconscious form models of representation of the things that can surprise us when reality is revealed to us.

Some people mistakenly call this the mental model or mindset. It is inaccurate because a mindset leads to actual behaviors, that is, actions, while archetypes lead to mental attitudes.

In the behavior encouraged by the mindset, if a person understands that they have the right to do something, they go there and do it; they simply act. In the attitude guided by the archetypes, if a person understands that they have the right to do something, they think before and react to the consequences of the act thought only in their mind. Whether or not the action will be carried out according to the person's thinking will depend on each person's mindset.

This becomes clearer when we understand that the imagination activates areas of the brain that are specialized in materializing a reality that only exists in each person's mind. At that moment the fantasy becomes real and the possibilities are endless. Archetypes help with this complex task, as they act as shortcuts to the things that can emerge from our imagination.

For example, when we say "mother", tenderness, kindness and safety usually come to mind. When we think of a dog, we usually remember a faithful and companion animal. If we talk about Mother Teressa of Calcutta what comes to us is kindness.

The simplest things have the ability to make us travel to fantastic places and alternative realities that encourage us to always want more and more. Leonardo knows this as well as anyone. He exercises this exhaustively every day. He is an avid reader of books in which he searches from adventure stories, to fiction, poetry, novels... with them, Leonardo exercises his mind in all the possibilities that are presented to him.

In the constant exercise of imagination and the discovery of alternatives that the mind can provide, Leonardo usually travels through his thoughts through the possibilities that may arise, even if in an alternative reality.

But, hang on! No need to be surprised! Leonardo is not a maniac who is hallucinating, imprisoning himself in a world that is his alone, as in a paranoid schizophrenia that makes the person lose the link with reality.

Everything is a great imaginative exercise. How to present Filomena, and how will this presentation influence Leonardo's colleagues? This is a doubt in his mind that needs to be exercised.

The most curious thing about our imagination is that we manage to get whole trips through our mind and thoughts in just a few seconds. If all the details were told, they would take several pages. Leonardo does this a lot: he exercises different situations in his imagination, searching in each one, which will be the most appropriate. It is the power of archetypes!

Chapter 4 - The presentation

↓

— Ladies and gentlemen, Filomena's house!

And the drums roll ...

Ra ta ta ...

Ra ta ta ...

Ra ta ta ... Ra ta ta ... Ra ta ta ...

Leonardo always wanted to do it that way. As on a stage, with special lights and spotlights valuing each moment.

— And now, ladies and gentlemen, I want to introduce you to Filomena's little house!

Ra ta ta ... ta ta ...

Ra ta ta ta ta ta ...

Ra ta ta ...

"She's a star, she is beautiful, her predominant color is of coffee with milk, but I will let her show everything to you, after all, no one better than the legitimate owner of all this to present her luxurious house with all the wealth of details that this requires, because we are talking about Filomena's house.", — an idyllic suspense begins and expresses a feeling in Leonardo of none other than Goethe[22].

THE VIOLET

UPON the mead a violet stood,
Retiring, and of modest mood,

In truth, a violet fair.
Then came a youthful shepherdess,
And roam'd with sprightly joyousness,
And blithely woo'd

With carols sweet the air

"Ah!" thought the violet, "had I been
For but the smallest moment e'en

Nature's most beauteous flower,
'till gather'd by my love, and press'd,
When weary, 'gainst her gentle breast,
For e'en, for e'en

One quarter of an hour!"

Alas! alas! the maid drew nigh,
The violet failed to meet her eye,

She crush'd the violet sweet.
It sank and died, yet murmur'd not:
"And if I die, oh, happy lot,
For her I die,

And at her very feet!"

Johann Wolfgang von Goethe

At that moment, Leonardo carefully places his hand deep in the right pocket of his jacket and takes out the small, fragile, sweet, docile and elegant Filomena. She was very quiet all the time … very calm … cozy and curled up … at the bottom of the jacket pocket.

…

The sound of a scratched record takes us out of the mental flow that was setting in after Goethe.

…

— At last, huh Leo! I thought you were not going to stop with that blah, blah, blah… Oh and before I forget, thank you very much for the presentation! — says Filomena in her firm soprano voice and makes a slight bow.

— Phew… I couldn't take it anymore! Well, it's true, I was cozy, and I was also very quiet, this is all true, but there is a reason for it: I was protecting my sensitive nose. I've told you more than once that I don't like the perfume on your clothes. It makes my nose itchy! — shouted Filomena, blowing her nose scandalously.

— I'm sorry, Filomena. But my mother … — Leonardo started speaking, trying to explain himself, when he is abruptly interrupted by Filomena.

— Okay, okay, okay! I know! Your mom loves putting on those products that make your clothes smell 'good' and you're not to blame. I told you, your mother is overprotective. She overdoes these cleaning things and makes your clothes all fluffy and scented... blah blah blah! — comments Filomena, making no reservations about exposing her discomfort.

— But okay! All right! So, how is it? Can I enter my little house now? Or is there something still missing? I see it is already done and set up. Can I enter? I need to eat my morning seeds and do my exercises. You don't want to have a stressed, overweight hamster, do you, Leonardo? Come on ... What are you waiting for? Put me there. There in the main access. On that bottom area. I can't start showing my house from my bedroom, right? I have secrets there! — says Filomena, giving specific guidance on how she wants to start the walkthrough.

— Oh, and before I forget. What was that idea about telling your mother that you're having a social experiment with me? I do not understand! Will you use me as an object in a social experiment? Is that right? You and I didn't agree about that! Do you know if I, by any chance, want to take part in your experiment? — Filomena amended sharply, imposing herself.

— Okay, sorry, my princess! — replied Leonardo, quite embarrassed!

— Wow ... you can stop with these intimacies! My name is Filomena! FI-LO-ME-NA! Don't give me that 'princess'! Let's keep it formal here. We are good colleagues, coworkers, that's all. And besides, we're in your office, aren't we? If you start with these intimacies and nicknames, what will people think? — Filomena's called out, putting things in their proper places. — And be aware that I will still think about whether I want to participate in your social experiment, but only after having my breakfast, okay? — Filomena imposed herself again, showing who is in charge there.

— Right then ... — said Leonardo, a little annoyed!

— Okay then ... nha, nha, nha ... — Filomena said. — Put me at the entrance at once, Leonardo! Carefully, please! — she ordered.

— Let's start here then ... hmm, hmm, hmmm ... — she prepared her little throat.

— I present you my Workstation here in the office... I can call my house like that, right Leonardo? After all, we are in an office and here the place where people work is called the Workstation, right? — asks Filomena.

— Yes, of course! This is your Workstation, Filomena! I did my best here to give you only the best — says Leonardo proudly.

— Okay, okay, Leonardo. You can leave it to me now! So, as I was saying, Leo... I mean, Leonardo, wanted to do this beauty for me because I was getting a little bored at home, you know? The whole day over there ... kind of just laying around ... killing time ... just with my basic little life ... most of the time alone ... just eating seeds, exercising, bathing in the sand bath, having some fun ... I was getting kind of depressed, you know? And there's also that nosy Boris. A pug dog that... — Filomena started amending, when Leonardo interrupted her.

— Filomena ... please! Can we skip that part and go ahead at once? — Leonardo called her attention, because she is impossible and has a real annoyance with Boris.

— COME ON, LEONARDO! No pressure! Oh my gosh! How bossy you are! Are you like that with all the people who work here in the office too? Wow ... well, whatever. Ah! For those who don't know English slang very well, 'whatever' generally means that any outcome is acceptable, but in this context, I used it as "it doesn't matter", ok?

— Well ... Continuing ... Here is the main entrance to my house, better, my Workstation, in fact it is the only one, and in this case it is this small transparent orange tunnel, which only lets me in, but does not let me go out. I already told Leonardo that I will want a small door that allows me to go out too, but up there, next to the leisure area. But so far, no progress, right, Mr. Leonardo? — Filomena says, following up on her orders.

— Well, maybe we can see that later, Filomena, please? — Leonardo intervened, otherwise an endless discussion would begin.

— Leonardo, Leonardo ... I'm just watching you collect promises and more promises ... I'm going to ask for all of them, huh? — Filomena warned, speaking very seriously.

— Well, after I enter the orange tube, I'm already on the balcony. I like to come here when I want to look at things from a different angle. The view is quite wide. I can see people from a very funny perspective from the bottom up, ha ha ha... well, this is the lowest part of my Workstation. From here I can go straight to the gym, and for that I need to climb this long lime green tube to my left. Now, if I'm hungry, like now, for example, I can go to the pantry. Follow me ... The access is through this other yellow tube, in the center. My meals are served there. Always balanced with carefully selected seeds. I have a very sensitive stomach, you know? — said Filomena, already speeding things up a little more. She is hungry!

— Now if I am really in the mood for a more exciting activity, I can take this automatic elevator and go straight to the leisure area, up there, where I can enjoy a very colored ball pit and next to it is my dance floor. Everything is automatic, just enter and the elevator goes up. When I get up there, everything is automatic too, because as soon as I enter it, my playlist starts to play, and the disco ball starts to spin. It's really cool! I'm a starlet after all, remember? — said Filomena, excited with the possibilities. — Ah, and on my playlist, I really like the upbeat, energizing, fast-paced songs! — she amends, excited.

— Right. Now I'm going to the kitchen, because I'm hungry! Follow me, as I climb this blue tube here in the center... I turn further up... I roll to the right... then to the left and *voilà* ... I reach the kitchen. Ah, for those who are not versed in French, "*voilà*" means "it's here". — completes Filomena, without hiding the disappointment when arriving at the pantry.

— Hey, Leonardo. What joke is this? Where's my meal? Do you want to see me malnourished, cadaverous, starving? I'll have to report you to the APA. Ah, for those who do not know or are not versed in these advanced acronyms, APA is the Animal

Protection Agency. Ah, for those who don't know what an acronym is ... — Leonardo interrupts her!

— Filomena! Enough of the show, please! Calm down, I brought your meal, I just haven't put it in the pantry yet! Calm down! Can you wait just a little bit? — said Leonardo, to calm the naughty girl, while calling his advisor Luana.

— Luana, please, can you give me that little box that I asked you to bring in earlier today from my car? Asked Leonardo, kindly.

— Hmmm... who is this? Luana, is it? Pretty brunette she huh? Green eyes ... — Filomena says, wanting to understand the relationship between Luana and Leonardo.

— Filomena, please don't make me feel ashamed. She's my Personal Assistant, co-worker, okay? That's all! — Leonardo said, half whispering.

— Well ... Here's your well-balanced meal, with a mix of five types of seeds and spectacular nutrients. — Leonardo formally announced, easing the situation.

— Fine! Thank you! And now excuse me for a few minutes? I'm going to eat some seeds. It's quick. We hamsters are fast and very accelerated. Just a few minutes and we will continue the tour, okay? Just a moment ... — said Filomena, eating her breakfast with five types of seeds and spectacular nutrients.

— Sorry guys. Filomena is very moody and was a little stressed this morning, you know? But she will get better as soon as she finishes her breakfast. — said Leonardo, quite embarrassed.

— I CAN HEAR EVERYTHING, LEONARDO ... — Filomena said, loudly as she nibbled her seeds.

— Well, let's give her a little privacy and we'll be right back to continue the tour, okay? — said Leonardo, to the excited people who wanted to hear much more from Filomena.

↑

Chapter 5 - Filomena

Leonardo has a very prodigious mind.

He is not sure if the previously thought-out approach is the best one to introduce Filomena to his colleagues, and he also knows that if he makes her too comfortable, it will be a mess, and may even frighten some people. The characteristics of originality, spontaneity and agitation of Filomena can bother anyone who is not used to seeing such a restless animal running in a crazy way through its colored tubes, corridors and doing activities in its exercise wheel, having fun in the ball pit, using an elevator, dancing on a private dance floor and everything. A highly playful space ... stimulating ... interactive ... magical!

Leonardo is also a little afraid of his own reaction when receiving criticism, comments or observations from his colleagues and how he will reply to those in a straight and unfiltered manner. To retake the creative essence, people's spontaneity needs to be recovered. Lack of objectivity has no place in this new order.

However, before all this, Leonardo is really questioning whether all this frenzy that caused his colleagues and other people in the company may be a sign of an alert for him to step back and put it all aside. That maybe he should put everything away and leave.

He also sees the other side; if on the contrary, this would not be a real green light for him to take advantage of the impact created and make a big turnaround that propels his desire to transform starting with the step of drawing people's attention to raise awareness, which he just managed to achieve.

Because the question that is actually on Leonardo's mind now is: "But what gives me the right to impose on my colleagues, my Director, and everyone as a matter of fact, such an unusual approach to stimulate their imagination and creativity in the company, including myself in this endeavor? Do they want it, need it and accept it?".

Of course! Leonardo did not ask in advance if they wanted something unusual to stimulate their minds, if they are dissatisfied with something, if they want to change their level of happiness at work. He is in fact, pushing everyone too far.

But at the same time Leonardo asks himself: "... if I do not take this initiative, someone, at some point, by some chance of fate, will really be concerned with seeking to improve the way the work is done? To make human relations within the company better and that this is reflected directly in their own relationship with work?".

The doubts that are filling Leonardo's mind are important to force reasoning and seek alternative paths and new possibilities, that is, to innovate.

The doubts themselves are not bad … even worse is to make a good decision.

When Filomena is projected in Leonardo's mind and this is done considering what the perspective of a small hamster would be, she turns into a starlet. She is a being that has a primordial behavior with much to teach. Her needs, her search for constant activity and the realization of her own meaning for her brief existence, which boils down to eating, exercising and reproducing.

A small being that is simple by its very nature, but when it is seen from our human perspective it can gain a meaning of a higher complexity, being able to convey teachings and lead to thoughts that by Leonardo's mind gain fantastic contours. His challenge is to make his colleagues realize this in a simple way.

In the thoughts that he secretly makes in his mind, flashes of situations that he would demand of himself appear in the form of Filomena's own voice speaking to him, as if she were Leonardo's alter ego[23].

This way, Leonardo takes the perspective of the little hamster that is now quiet eating her little seeds. He observes her and ponders on his thoughts ... on what she would be like talking about him to people, in an interview, as if in one of those characters in documentaries in which testimonials are given.

— Finally, some peace to eat my little seeds. I need to eat them very carefully. Oh, so hungry! — Filomena would say, following her feeding instinct for survival.

— I'll talk to you now. But keep it between us, okay? For real! I like Leo! He cleans my house, gives me food, takes care of my health, my safety, my comfort, and he cares about me. — Filomena would say, because she would care about me.

— But he is a bit hard to understand sometimes. What was he thinking? To bring me here to the office to work with him every day as if I were some kind of hero for his problems here at the company. I help him with his paranoias, no problem, but that should happen at home! Now, to bring me here to the company? I found it very daring on his part. He will end up finding trouble! Furthermore, I think he already found it and it was not a small one! —

Filomena would say, without holding back, pulling my ear!

— Oh, please! Okay, I know, I must see the positive side of things. At least I don't have to spend all day putting up with Boris. He is a cute dog, but mischievous! He even tried to mark his territory at the base of my house, back at home! That is my territory. There, I am the star! He's just... a little dog, really! — Filomena would vent.

— But I understand Leo. Poor thing! He has some difficulty understanding or accepting certain things or concepts. But I'm showing him the best I can. At least from my hamster perspective, which, by the way, is far superior to the capacity of an executive in his position. — mocked Filomena, remembering that a primordial being can perceive much more than a human being.

↑

But the real big question that bothers Leonardo is to clarify these doubts and explain to his colleagues how the observation of a small hamster in an artificial habitat could transform his own daily life, that of his colleagues, his General Director and the company as a whole.

For example, from the primordial being view, a hamster in its little house will look for the rest area when it is tired, the eating area when it is hungry, the exercise area when it is excited, and the rest of the areas as it explores that microverse created there. These will be the animal's responses to the stimuli it receives from the environment, called stimulus responses[24]. This will be so and will not change, for it is part of the nature of this little animal. It is their instinct and they will always respond like that.

If we look at how the responses to stimuli happen in a business organization, they are also subject to similar phenomena and will respond to them on an incentive basis while maintaining a pattern. What changes is the complexity of the related events.

For example, the phenomenon that represents what companies constantly seek, that is, to obtain good results and profit. This will be achieved when the company has adequate resources that represent the least possible risk to its operation. The variables in this equation are the resources themselves and the risks inherent to their application.

If the company does not find the appropriate resources to accomplish its purpose, — also known as delivering value — with a level of risk that is acceptable to itself and thus obtaining the results it strives for, it can decide to simply stop its product or service offering that aren't fitting in the equation. To fine-tune the balance of risk versus result, the company can choose resources that reduce risks by hiring better qualified specialists, for example. There is also the possibility to transfer the risks to third parties. This is usually done through insurance or an outsourcing contract. All are ways to persist, in order to proceed with the business.

From the perspective of a primordial being, how would this be perceived and treated? In this case, by Filomena.

↓

— We hamsters, for example, have no problem with resources, as it is all very simple! Important resources are those that allow us to survive. Everything else is superfluous, therefore, totally liable to be discontinued or replaced immediately. — Filomena would say, about hamster subsistence, explaining the difference between resources and superfluous resources.

— Regarding the risks, if we are in nature, we stay in our dens to protect ourselves from predators and the weather. When we are in captivity, the greatest risks are stress and for that we have the exercise wheel. It is not superfluous, because we need to release the energy of our excitement or we freak out and start to bite everything, even our owner. It's part of our hamster essence to be and act like that. — Filomena reminds about a component of its primordial nature; whose life expectancy is approximately three and a half years.

↑

Still from the perspective of a more fundamental view, for some companies good results go far beyond pure and simple profit! For them, the results will be considered good when they manage to combine a combination of direct and indirect benefits for everyone involved in the process. Customers, suppliers, employees, shareholders, service providers, society and natural resources. The entire ecosystem needs to benefit from it, or the result of the equation will not matter. Profiting for profiting is too small and limited...

Regarding this aspect and from the primary perspective of an executive, how would this be perceived and dealt with? In this case, according to Leonardo's mind it's in the eyes of Filomena.

↓

"Although, on second thought, this way of seeing results can be difficult to get into the minds of many company directors out there. I think that my General Director may be among those, but that's the way it is, not everything can be as we would like to", reflects

Leonardo, between his thoughts that oscillate through Filomena's primordial perspective and his own.

— Another thing that Leo doesn't seem to understand very well, but his mother understands very well, is that in the world of hamsters a good result consists of a spacious house, fluffy bedding so that we can curl up in it, be able to move around through challenging paths and corridors that take us in all directions, having space to exercise, good food, a good rest area and of course, the possibility to reproduce. This is part of our essence. So, we feel good, the companies that manufacture our houses are good, the people who make our food and medicines are good, we manage to be happy and we make our owners happy. — Filomena would teach, considering what a good result is for her, from the perspective of a hamster.

"So, companies that work like that, that is, that maintain full responsibility in relation to good results, will only have this behavior if their governing body thinks like that and acts like that. Since it is difficult to get that into the head of my General Director; the fault is not with the company, nor with the employees, but with its management. If the General Director does not encourage and support her employees to celebrate the results of the achievements obtained in all areas, it is not because the company did not want to, but because it is not looking at things with responsibility so that the feeling of achievement is highlighted.", reflects Leonardo, disturbed by what he perceives from people in the company.

— A hamster usually has only two owners during its life, which is actually extremely short compared to human life, about less than 4% on average. The first owner is the one who takes care of our breeding in captivity for trade and the second is the one who buys us to be their pet. During this period, if the second owner does not take care of us properly, maintaining all the care so that our artificial environment has a good result for us, we have no option, we are left with a high level of stress and we chew at everything that is within our reach. — Filomena would remind, about the fate and primordial behavior of a hamster.

"So, from this perspective, I need to make my General Director understand once and for all that companies need everything, absolutely everything, to be in control. Only then will things work well. Things need to work and be in balance. Although this balance is maintained artificially. No problem! You just need everything to work well! For example, when I brought my little Filomena and her house here, without talking to my General Director, regardless of how forced this attitude was on my part, I am finding trouble so that all of us in the company can leave our comfort zone in which we settled and start to see, as an organization, new ways to transform our operation. We need people to be happy when creating new things or stagnation will set in irreversibly.", ponders Leonardo in his thoughts.

↑

Leonardo's mind is still racing to find the best way to approach Filomena and her house in the face of the situation he created. How would he present all that? What challenges would he bring to his colleagues and the company as a whole? How can this rich universe that represents primordial thought and metaphorical parallels gain meaning in understanding the organizational ecosystem?

↓

— Filomena! Have you finished? Can we continue the tour? — said Leonardo, with a positive tone.

— Yes, Leonardo. We can! I'll start where we left off before my break, okay? Well, after having my meal here in the kitchen I have several options: I can go back to the balcony or go to the shower room or take the elevator to the leisure area. Hamsters love to bathe, but it's a sand bath and not water. In fact, we don't like to get wet, you know? Shall we go to the shower room? — invites, Filomena.

— Oops ... – Leonardo slips, unintentionally.

— Oops? What oops? Leonardo! Where's the sand bath in my bathroom? Haven't you brought it yet? Leonardo, this can't go on! You forget my most basic needs, Leonardo! I'm a starlet, Leonardo! Do you want me to have my hair wrinkly and ugly? Do you? — said Filomena, raging and chattering her teeth. Hamsters do this when they are nervous.

— Do you know why that happened, Filomena? Since you will be coming home with me every day in the late afternoon, you can have your bath at home, much more comfortably. — said Leonardo, trying to ease and settle the situation.

— I'll think about it, but it doesn't mean I already agreed, okay? We'll talk about that later! Well, let's continue then... Leaving the pantry through the only possible exit that is not to the balcony, or to the bathroom, which is incomplete... where are we going to get then? Come on... Ah! In the gym! Nice! Here you can see my aerobic exercise wheel. I love spending time here. When I'm at the wheel my mind wanders, thinking about life, philosophizing about the hamster way of being, finding answers to the problems that Leo... — said Filomena, when Leonardo interrupted her.

— Well, Filomena, let's leave that alone, right? Don't you want to show your room? — interrupted Leonardo, a little awkwardly.

— That's right! Now, going down to this more reserved area, I follow this very long, straight red tube and get to my bedroom. Here I have this bed with fluffy bedding where I can curl up and rest, after all, all stars need to rest and I'm a simple hamster! I need to rest between my meals and my aerobic activities. When I'm around, I tend to meditate and reflect on the hamster problems that come up. There are so many! If I'm going to eat, if I'm going to exercise, if I'm going to the dance floor, if I'm going to the bathroom, if I'm going to chew on something to make my teeth the right size, if I'm going to explore the outside world and take some risks, live some adventures ... — begins to wander Filomena.

— And taking this elevator I have access to this other part here where the leisure area is. I really enjoy spending time here. It has a colored ball pit that is very fun and the dance floor with lighting and an awesome playlist ... — Filomena shows off.

— Well that's it! This is my little house, but here in the office is my Workstation. — said Filomena, already ending the tour.

— And the rest, Filomena? — asked Leonardo, wanting her to continue.

— Okay, okay, Leonardo. If you insist! Well, there's this other area coming down from my room. I will go through this pink tube that is where I satisfy my physiological needs. It's the bathroom! There is this sand that is very cute, and this is where... well, nothing new. And connected to my room at the top, there is the penthouse, which, as I am seeing, is still without the exit I asked for, right Leonardo? — highlights Filomena, without beating around the bush.

— We'll solve this exit at a later time. Thank you, Filomena. Very informative the tour of your workstation. — said Leonardo, ending the presentation.

— Later, later... this later has a name, Mr. Leonardo, it's called procrastination. But ok, for now! We'll talk about it later when we get home! Okay? Well ... you're welcome! I'll be here, but just reminding that you still have much bigger problems to solve than my bathroom and my exit door on the penthouse. Good luck! — Filomena finished.

↑

Leonardo with his prodigious mind did the reflective exercise. The possibilities of introducing Filomena and her house are many. He wants to use this to encourage people in the company to look at everything around them. Could doing this in a simpler and more direct manner be the best way out? His challenge is to find answers that are both simple and straightforward to the challenges of everyday corporate life.

Chapter 6 - General director

Leonardo has been to his General Director's office many times. He never had a permanent, recurring agenda or anything. Whenever he needed alignment on a specific matter, he would show up there and talk, usually on very quick schedules.

Her office is quite ample with just over 1000 sq. ft. When any subject is brought up there to be discussed, it seems that the room gets small in the face of how magnified the subjects get when they are discussed with Teressa.

The decoration of the room is sober. There is an abstract art picture on the wall behind the General Director's desk, panels with phrases from modern and contemporary management gurus are strategically scattered on the walls and there are also a few discreet decorative objects with contemporary inspiration around. Natural light highlights this sobriety while revealing the striking and impeccable organization and cleanliness of the environment as a whole.

At another table next to Teressa's desk, awards are lined up in recognition of business and professional excellence. They are trophies and plaques collected over the more than twenty years dedicated to the company. You can also see books, many of them received as gifts. Picture frames are also part of the decoration with photos where she is next to celebrities from the corporate world in which she participates. Most were taken during her trips to events, awards, and other honors received from business and professional entities.

In a corner of the room there is a counter with coffee, tea, water, juices and cookies. Self-service! The environment as a whole is warm and friendly. And the aroma, the same as the reception, is soft, soothing and very pleasant.

In this climate of balance, tranquility, peace and harmony, a volcano appears to erupt, bringing alongside an earthquake that makes the building's twenty-five floors tremble, when the General Director's Executive Assistant, Miss Stella, brings the news of what Leonardo did and the repercussions already identified inside and outside the company.

"It is already almost 11 am of a workday that started just before 8:30 am and I see that my General Director is facing a very busy Monday. And now you will have to deal with this situation more. I suspected that Leonardo was up to something. When he left here earlier today, after talking to Teressa, he didn't want to open up with me. My recommendation for him not to pursue any new exploits seems to have had no effect. Well, if not even the General Director's direct order made him change his course of action, it would not be my recommendation that would have that effect.", thought Miss Stella, while Teressa, upset, thought of drastic attitudes towards Leonardo.

— Miss Stella, I do not believe that Leonardo had the audacity to not follow my guidance! Is he going crazy? Does he need to see a therapist? I don't know ... that boy just keeps finding trouble! With so many things I have to solve. I can't be everywhere all the time. After all, that is why I have coordinators, supervisors, managers and many good employees, and it is worth noting, all with salaries well above the market average... They are there to solve whatever is necessary, not to get me into more trouble! — says Teressa quite shaken.

— Calm down, Teressa! I'm sure he didn't do it out of spite! Young executives are really inventive! They want to transform everything they touch. And Leonardo already has a history of achievements here at the company. He certainly has his reasons for what he did. It's cultural. — pondered Miss Stella, trying to calm the General Director's spirits.

— Cultural? Cultural? And the culture and image of our company, how is it going to look? And how am I going to handle this now? Everything is already on the company's intranet. Look here ... Look ... — she says showing the screen of her smartphone. — This situation is the pits! Look at these hashtags:

#BraveManager #Filomena #CrazyManager #NewToy #Workaholic #FilomenaChallenge #TheAmazingFilomena ... I don't understand anything!

— And what is that about Filomena? Leonardo is deranged in his ideas, it is not possible... — shouts Teressa, incredulous in what she is seeing.

— The whole thing can be bigger than we think, because it's already on the Internet too, Teressa. It has already crossed outside the company's intranet barrier! — said Miss Stella.

— What? You mean it is visible outside the company too? On the Internet? — she asked incredulously.

— Yes, that's right!

— I can't believe it... — she says as she opens social networks on her smartphone and sees that they are flooded with messages talking about Leonardo. — It's true, look, here! Oh, my goodness! I already have messages from some business friends asking me if the new feature will be open to public visitation! Oh, I'm so mad at Leonardo! I'm already a joke! — snapped Teressa, at this moment a joke between friends and colleagues.

— Oh, and there is a live streaming too ... — adds Miss Stella, to complete.

— Live... there's even a live streaming?! Let me see... where? — Teressa searches erratically on social media on her smartphone. — Look, a live streaming coming from our offices... we are live for everyone, being a joke... look there, look there... it's Leonardo... and there are a lot of employees looking at what he is doing. What is he doing? What's that in his hand? He's got something in his hand! What is that? A mouse? Miss Stella, but what madness is this? He went crazy... — she threw herself in her office chair, close to having a nervous breakdown.

— Teressa, let's stay calm, okay? I am also stunned by Leonardo's attitude and the repercussions he is causing, but I'm sure we can turn it all in our favor, you can bet. I have some ideas. Let's think together a little bit and everything will be right. — said Miss Stella trying to calm Teressa down, who got clearly disturbed, something easy to trigger due to her delicate emotional balance.

— I'll show him something! When I catch him, I will ... — continued Teressa, when she was interrupted by Miss Stella.

— In fact, I strongly recommend that nothing be done now. Calm, elegance and serenity is what we need in this moment and for the next steps. — recommended Miss Stella, concerned with the consequences that fervent acts might trigger, further worsening the situation as a whole and the company's image.

Miss Stella is cunning and can see ahead. Her way of looking at a situation is holistic and integrated, just like Leonardo's.

"Until this moment, nobody knows that Leonardo was instructed not to continue with this initiative. Only Teressa, Leonardo, me and probably Lucy know that. We may use this restricted information to our advantage and to protect the company. The disruptive initiatives that Teressa also implemented in the past may be a good background set up to use in this situation.", carefully thought Miss Stella, in an approach suggestion that could help flatten the crisis beginning to take shape.

— Fine! Fine! I'll calm down! Please, Miss Stella, fetch me a glass of sugar water and tell Leonardo to come to my office. Let's talk and fix this at once. Oh, and ask him to bring that pet with him too. I want to see what he has to say about all of this! Give me at least fifteen minutes to recompose myself. Oh, and before I forget, transfer my last appointments of this morning to the afternoon. — asked Teressa to Miss Stella.

Alone in her office, she begins to reflect ...

"Wow, how I suffer with Leonardo. It is very difficult to find resources that can solve the difficult equation of obtaining results. Dealing with people is very complex. But I know why. Unlike machines, equipment and automation systems, people can think. The problem, to my despair, and in everything there is always at least one (problem), is the way some people think. It is not always beneficial or is well aligned with what we seek in companies. Finding good employees who are apt for certain types of work is a huge challenge. Sometimes who really should have to think, does not think or thinks incorrectly, and those who should not need to think much, in fact shouldn't even think, but only do what is expected of them according to the company's processes, insist on thinking... ", reflects, Teressa about the complexity of her role.

"How difficult... it is a complex equation, but it is part of my mission as General Director. CEO, what a powerful and intimidating acronym. Chief Executive Officer. Look at what I got myself into when I left my tranquil previous position about five years ago as the General Director of Marketing and Products and took on this challenge here: Being the main position of the organization and responsible for the implementation of existing plans and policies, ensuring the successful business management and defining the future strategy.", she continued to reflect.

"In short, I just need to ensure that the organizational guidelines are followed so that everything works well, managing crises of all kinds and, of course, trying not to freak out in the process. The biggest problem is that part of the basic profile of a good human resource needs to balance elements as diverse as the ability to think critically, the willingness to work, have the necessary technical skills, have some professional experience and be able to utilize all this set of skills and competencies to bring the results we need, but I think this is still not the worst... ", she considers, about the profile of the company's professionals.

"There is also the issue of (in)dependence and the ability to act under certain guidelines. In my experience, I always thought that more independent people could be excellent for complex positions and situations, while more dependent people would be better at following processes.", she thought about the profile she perceives in Leonardo and Miss Stella.

"Over the years here at the company, I have observed that this is not a general rule. I realize that independent people can be excellent at executing more rigid processes. I think this is due to the fact that they have a view that tends to be more critical about things. They can more easily perceive the interdependencies that are present in the processes, which are very sensitive and that is why they know the importance behind them and try hard to follow everything to the letter. I would bet my career on that!", she thinks about the profiles she likes to have by her side.

"On the other hand, I have seen that dependent people show a tendency to be much more rigid on issues related to indicators and the fulfillment of well-defined steps. So, they do very well when it comes to facing challenges that require complex orchestrations.", analyzes Teressa, reflecting on the challenges of roles in the company.

— Miss Stella, I can't determine which profile Leonardo fits into. While he is independent in his thoughts, the department he manages is the one that best follows the processes and has the lowest rate of non-conformities. However, about following guidelines... he is not a good example. We need our guidelines to be respected. This is very important to the company... it is an important condition that we cannot give up. — argues, Teressa.

— See, for example, how much we had to invest in human and financial resources to define and consolidate our mission, vision and values that underlie our corporate strategy. Then, to evolve our processes... it was also a huge effort and investment. Now Leonardo comes again and ignores all of that. I don't understand this guy... it's as if he were telling everyone that these things don't matter... — Teressa thinks out loud in a rhetorical description, wanting to approach the company's situation, trying to understand why Leonardo acts in this manner.

— I already told Lucy, Leonardo's Personal Assistant. I told her to ask him to come in about twenty minutes. — informed Miss Stella, interrupting Teressa's rhetorical flow.

— Miss Stella, please sit here. Let's try to think together on what we will do to overcome this chaotic situation that is installed. — asked Teressa, now a little less upset.

— You said earlier that you had some ideas on how to reverse all this. Can you please share this with me? Let's see if you can help me find a way out of this madness. — said Teressa.

Chapter 7 - The change of strategy

At the university attended by Miss Stella when she was young and in which she concluded her graduation in Business Administration, she was taught that there is no good or bad strategy, what can there be is the absence of strategy and when that happens the fate of the business and the company is being handed over to fate... to luck... and it is not possible to thrive in that scenario.

With that in mind, she always knew that for every situation and for any problem that arises, there will always be a solution. The difference between people who succeed and those who fail is knowing how to look at the solutions, not at the problems.

— Yes, Teressa. I thought of something here that can completely reverse the situation and put us on another level of positive image gain! — Miss Stella began her explanation.

— Well, my dear, you just got my full attention! What magic would you be suggesting us to do? — said Teressa, leaning back in her comfortable chair and relaxing, ready to listen to her faithful and insightful Executive Assistant.

As she leaned back, Teressa looked into Miss Stella's eyes and cast immense energy into that look to try to capture everything that could come out of there as an alternative to a new scenario. From her perspective ... well ... in fact, she didn't believe it would be possible to give an elegant solution to all that. She was already even contemplating subjecting Leonardo to a suspension, in addition to demanding a formal retraction from him to the whole company for the crazy things he did. Teressa is not a good example of flexibility when it comes to the guidelines she establishes. There was a time when she unilaterally ended a millionaire contract with one of her main suppliers because the Sales Executive of that company did not honor the anticipation of part of a batch of raw materials with which he had committed to deliver when closing the transaction.

— Teressa let's start from the facts and from what we know so far. Our company has a consolidated image of responsibility for delivering quality in everything it does. Our excellence is known and recognized by the Street. — continued, Miss Stella. — In order to achieve our excellent quality, credibility and excellence rates, we are constantly surpassing ourselves and this is also recognized by the Street, right? — asked Miss Stella rhetorically. Teressa nodded, while keeping fully focused on the explanation.

— So, Teressa, my recommendation is that we should take advantage of this identity of ours towards the Street to give an answer in that sense, that is, that we are posing a new challenge for our entire organization to respond, since we believe that we need to reinvent ourselves once again. — explained Miss Stella... and continued.

— The whole unusual scenario that Leonardo brought to us today has proven itself to work, because he triggered a real spontaneous movement inside the offices today that is echoing inside and outside our company. He is the Manager of the Marketing and Products Department and is directly responsible for our company to continue to be recognized as the best in everything new it presents to the market. In other words, it makes perfect sense that he is also the pivot of this great transformation. — completed Miss Stella.

— What we need now is to understand what Leonardo's real intentions are with what he brought here today. So let me ask you, Teressa! When he came here to talk to you earlier today, what exactly did he tell you? What did he explain to you?

— Well, first he said that his department has a completely stagnant creativity. He said that they haven't been able to present anything effectively innovative for a long time and needed to shock everyone's realities around there. — Teressa began to answer and continued.

— Then he said that he had decided to bring an artificial habitat here and that he would set it up right in the middle of his department, occupying a good part of the circulation area of the offices on the eighth floor, creating discomfort and extra care for everyone. He also said that it would be something like a Playful Space. Of course, it made me crazy, first because he did it without consulting me, and I had already told him not to do anything crazy again without talking to me before. Second, he brought here something that will disturb the workspace of the employees in his department, precisely where they need to be concentrated to develop our new products. — said Teressa, already changing her tone. And continued.

— And he didn't explain to me what he intended to do with everything he brought or even how it would help his team. Ah, for the record, I don't believe that our products are experiencing an innovation crisis. We are launching successful products year after year. The numbers show that. — said Teressa, thoughtful after saying it out loud. It looks like it didn't sound right.

— Well ... — began to ponder Miss Stella calmly and cautiously. — Maybe you didn't give Leonardo a chance to explain what he intends to do. Even because

I remember hearing you say a very loud and angry 'ENOUGH', or am I wrong?

— It is true, I was very upset because he had not previously shared his intentions with me, and I did not let him speak.

— Well, in that case, as soon as he gets here it seems like it's time to put this all on a new level of understanding and alignment, of course, if you understand that the strategy I proposed makes sense. — Said Miss Stella, cheerfully.

— Yes, it makes perfect sense. We will actually be looking for an innovative answer to continue creating innovative products! But we have to guide this conversation very well with Leonardo. He needs to be perfectly aligned with the message that we want to convey to everyone. Otherwise, we can cause the opposite effect. — amended Teressa, already having ideas on how to create new processes to reverse the situation of creative stagnation in the Marketing and Products department, thanks to the insight given by her advisor, Miss Stella.

— I want to take advantage of this and expand the agenda. Let's think about creating new disruptive environments here in the company with more decompression spaces. In addition to the hot tub, ping pong and pool tables, more play spaces for our employees to use. We will only need to put some rules in place so that people can have more flexibility in organizing their work areas, leaving them more personalized and connected with their preferences. We just cannot neglect and let them generate operational non-conformities. — Teressa was already deliberating, excited by the possibilities that were revealed in her mind.

Initially Teressa had a pessimistic, chaotic and disastrous view, in which she had rejected, destroyed, hated, slaughtered and buried Leonardo's proposal. Suddenly everything changed to a vision of maintaining the image of solidity, commitment and seriousness towards its employees, shareholders, customers and society.

The General Director would now try to take complete control of Leonardo's initiative, embodying what was once an original idea of rummaging through people's thinking structure in favor of a transformation based on everyone's sense of belonging, founded on the pursuit of happiness. Now, after being assimilated by the company, it would turn into something that would be imposed, from top to bottom, as an obligation to innovate and think outside the box.

This is the company's primary response. It makes its protective corporate cells phagocytize[25] the most authentic desire for innovation and transformation, assimilating these initiatives because it is necessary that it be in control, even if artificially, of the things that must happen. Again, Leonardo was right in his reflections.

The original essence of focusing on people's happiness so that, being so, they feel free to create and invent, now passes to a force of the organization in having in its hands total control of how things should happen. Innovation is instituted as a process.

The company needs everything to be under control, even if control is detrimental to the innovation process. You cannot truly innovate without people being happy, connected to their challenges and totally free from limiting processes. You can't innovate by decree or by process.

Leonardo knows that. He thinks about it and has his own strategy for making things work despite his General Director's intention. On behalf of the company, she needs to answer for how things should work. Yes, that stimulus response that Leonardo predicted.

— All right, Teressa. However, we don't know if this is what Leonardo is really looking for. — highlights Miss Stella, as she is looking further ahead.

— Why do you think that? Do you know something I don't know? Did Leonardo say anything to you? — asked Teressa sharply.

— When he was here earlier today, I tried to get additional information about what I wanted to talk to you about, but he didn't open anything else for me. It just reminded me of the actions he took in the past and the transformation proposals brought by him that culminated in many gains for the company, including the excellent growth indicators and even the move of the company's headquarters to this building where we are today. I felt that he was really determined to do something different.

— And after he left my office, did you talk to him?

— Yes, when he left your office, after your denial of his initiative, I realized that he was feeling down. Nothing more. He just said to me, "I'm going to pick up the rest of the dignity I have left and try to glue it back, piece by piece."

Part 2

Chapter 8 - Leonardo

Leonardo is a brilliant person.

But what defines a brilliant person? Someone who has intelligence above the average and is exceptional in just about everything they do? The high skills combined with the ability to achieve some competencies most people can take a lifetime to achieve and would still be at most good at it, but they would never be brilliant?

Just to exemplify, those who have absolute or perfect pitch, when learning the names of musical notes and their various scales, can instantly say what is the name of the musical note played, no matter the instrument, tone, timbre, intensity or pitch. People with this ability can tell what is the note emitted by the drop of rain when it falls on the ground, by the bark of a dog, by the wind that blows, by the human voice that speaks, that sings, that cries or that laughs... for people with absolute pitch all sounds have a value. Some of these people go even further and are able to reproduce the sequence of sounds they have just heard as if they were a digital recorder and can even play any song by ear on the instrument they master.

People like Leonardo may even be called brilliant, but I would add restlessness to their behavior, that is, they are not content with things continuing as they are, without improving, evolving, reframing and transforming. They expect people to evolve in their thoughts, ways of seeing and perceiving their own lives and everything that can orbit around them such as society, work, human relationships, survival and their own development!

Within the microverse Leonardo thought to present Filomena, his starlet, his alter ego, he seeks to enter a new field of possibilities, because his mind insists on going faster than his ability to articulate the actions resulting from his restlessness.

It is a characteristic of brilliant minds to find shortcuts to solve problems that non-brilliant minds cannot even conceive of as existing. The shortcuts simply reveal themselves. Contrary to what one might think, the speed that the brilliant mind travels through the shortcuts it sees is normal, but as they are shortcuts, they can lead to the result much faster. Non-brilliant people need to follow the conventional path of deductive thinking, follow the techniques they have learned and look at each intermediate step before the next one starts and so on. That way, it takes a lot longer to reach the result... that is, if they reach it!

For a brilliant person, the intermediate steps and their partial results are irrelevant because they know they are in the right direction, even if they do not know why they are.

↓

— Filomena... Filomena... FILOMENA! — Leonardo called, whispering loudly.

— Speak, Leo... what a lack of peace! I was here, resting. You know that after eating my little seeds I need to relax a little. Remember that I am a very fragile starlet who always needs to be very beautiful, rested and willing. — she replied, also half whispering.

— Do you think I'm going to be in trouble for bringing you here? I mean, I know I will have problems, but will they fight me or scold me and my colleagues who helped me today with the assembly of your Workstation? — asked Leonardo.

— Leo, you already know that answer very well! You don't have to consult me for that. Of course, your attitude will have consequences. In the world of hamsters, whenever one of us takes the other's seed, or invades the other's space, this creates stress and fights are started. Nothing deadly, but it happens. — mused Filomena. — And as for bringing problems to your colleagues, well it depends a lot on your company's policy. In our hamster coexistence code, anyone who disrespects the other's space and food is subject to attack, no matter who they are. You should have thought of that before doing the things you did, right? Ah! Listen! Why are we even whispering? — asked Filomena, curious.

— It's just that I don't want anyone to hear us! — justified Leonardo.

— Leo, nobody will hear us, it's just you and me here in your thoughts! Do not worry! — recalled Filomena.

↑

— Leonardo, Miss Stella warned me that the General Director wants to speak with you in twenty minutes. And she asked to bring Filomena along! — Lucy informed, a little worried about the consequences that could result from Leonardo's impetuous actions.

— Thank you, Lucy. I will prepare to go to the scaffold[26]. Will I be entitled to one last wish? Convicts generally have that right, don't they? — asked Leonardo, being dramatic, but in a surprisingly calm tone.

— Don't be dramatic, Leonardo. From the tone of Miss Stella, it seemed to me much more that it will be just an alignment conversation, after all you disrespected a direct determination from your General Director. And if it wasn't enough, the whole thing leaked on the Internet, there are videos and memes. They are already associating our company with #Filomena — completed Lucy, with some reservation, but calm. — Beyond the clamor, of course: everyone wants to meet Filomena. — she completed.

— Yeah... I know... I screwed up. And badly! — replied Leonardo, with his head down.

Lucy's complicity in this endeavor was no exception. She acts very much in line with Leonardo's thoughts and that was one more reason that made him have her as Personal Assistant. A really trustworthy person.

Leonardo's thoughts do not stop. Filomena is his provocative shadow in the most unusual thoughts.

— Listen to me, Leo. What are you doing, dude? You faced all this, had this crazy idea of bringing me here to stir people's spirits and now that you quite intensely managed to accomplish this, you will throw in the towel? No way... I will not allow that to happen! — Filomena shouted, calling out Leonardo's dignity.

— Wait a minute, I'm going up to my gym, because I think a lot better when I'm exercising. The increased quantity of oxygen in my little hamster brain makes me see things more clearly. Wait, I'll just slide over here... ah... what a thrill... let's go! — said

Filomena, entering her exercise wheel and beginning to move on it.

— Look, my dear Leo! What are you afraid of? What do you think of your performance here at the company? What bothers you? — provokes Filomena, without holding back.

— Filomena, I am part of a very good organization, but it has a plaster cast on some things. Do you know that maxim about the well-known mission, vision and values trilogy being at the base of the strategic definitions that are drawn up by organizations in general? — says Leonardo, irritated.

— Yes, of course I know... In fact, I was the one who demanded it at home. In the last review we made of it, less than two months ago, our mission was to be the happiest family we can, as long as we are together, our vision was to share this mission with as many families as possible, until the whole world knows of that and our founding values have been changed to respect and honesty. — said Filomena, without blinking.

— Well then, Filomena. Here is one of the problems: the company's mission, vision and values were defined when I was still a trainee. It is old, outdated, plastered, limiting and no longer represents our business reality, much less that of the society in which we are a part of. — lamented Leonardo, already victimizing himself.

— Just to give you an example, if we go back in time a little, towards the end of the 1990s, I think it was in 1997, when Steve Jobs returned to resume his executive position at Apple, a slogan was created at the time for the company: "Think Different".

Filomena was paying attention, while accelerating the speed of her activity on the exercise wheel.

— So, the meaning, what was at the base of that Apple slogan was a double vision: internally, for everyone who worked there, there was a mission to think differently from everything that had already been thought to create the unusual. Thus came iMac, iPod, iTunes, iPhone, iPad and a whole generation of devices and services that simply transformed the way people relate to mobile technology and online services. On the other hand, the same slogan was an explicit message to users. The vision was for them to leave the old behind once and for all and embrace a new paradigm. This led to value, to creating a relationship with mobile, personal, and cloud computing technologies. After that, Apple has changed its trilogy a lot of times. — Leonardo reflected on his pain points. — Well, then, Filomena, the mission, vision and values trilogy should not be something crystallized in time that works as a kind of corporate straitjacket for organizational guidelines. It must be continually reconstructed, reframed and rethought. If the mission does not adapt throughout the evolution of society itself, properly aligned with the strategic vision of the organization and its values, the trend is none other than stagnation. — vented Leonardo.

— I agree with you on everything Leo. But what about people? What do you think they want? What do your colleagues here at the company want? What do they dream of? In our hamster world all we care about is being well and happy. As long as we do not lack physical activity, enough room to live and places to explore, delicious seeds and clean sand bath, we will always be fine. — explained Filomena.

— I'm always in doubt, Filomena. Is it all just a latent desire of people to conquer and maintain a professional position that meets their most basic and common requirements in a system where competitiveness between professionals is decisive? Do they think only of items such as wages above the market average, a good package of benefits, adherence and adequacy to their technical and academic training, consistency with their past experience, flexible workday where productivity is what really matters, reimbursement or full payment of courses for technical and personal improvement, in addition to participation in the company's financial results? Is that all they see or are they looking for something more? Are these requirements that my colleagues here at the company understand as the most important? For them, real happiness has no place in this equation, that is, the person feels happy with what they do, and in what they work for? — shoots Leonardo, while Filomena accelerates her exercise wheel even more.

— But what would that happiness be, Leonardo? For us hamsters the happiness is to be in balance between food and physical well-being. And for you humans, what is it? — provoked Filomena.

— What I have noticed is that the predominant counterpart has been these monetary, assistance and maintenance of personal or family comfort. — says Leonardo. — More relevant things like autonomy in the management of your decisions, the requirements directly linked to personal support for decision making within the most varied organizational contexts, the freedom to think collectively and creatively in new ways of doing things, satisfaction to be helping other people and society as a whole. It seems that these and others are not considered important or relevant here in this happiness package. — complements Leonardo, restless and anxious.

— Well, Leonardo. Each of us needs to feel useful. We hamsters feel useful when we are doing what makes us happy. It's so simple for us! You humans complicate things too much! — provokes Filomena, once again, baffling Leonardo.

— Feeling useful. Yes. And this seems to be much more of a commonsense expression than a therapeutic pursuit. But it is a very serious study. — says Leonardo, while Filomena accelerates the speed on the exercise wheel even more.

— I know that this has to do with the study of the so-called cognitive-behavioral therapy in which there is a search for understanding the balance between the cognitive triad and cognitive distortion. — recalled Leonardo, from his studies on the psychology of human behavior when in his Marketing course.

"In the cognitive triad, the goal is to see how deep the negative views a person has about himself. It goes through inadequacy first, i.e. I am uninteresting; I am a boring person. Then it goes through the negative view of the world in relation to work, i.e. people do not appreciate my work. Finally, the negative view of the future, i.e. I will never be happy.", recalls Leonardo, who in addition to being a manager is versed in human behavioral psychology.

"In cognitive distortion, the challenge is to determine what leads people to mistakenly anticipate the conclusions they draw about themselves and their potential. The structuring of personal experiences in an absolute and inflexible way leads to misinterpretations regarding personal performance and the judgment of external situations.", he continues to remember the concepts, brilliantly.

"It is very common for people who are unhappy to jump to conclusions about their performance based on little evidence and still choose only those that are negative. Thus, it tends to generalize that everything from then on will be bad or negative. This characteristic of human behavior is exploited by marketing in advertising to encourage cognitive distortion by making people consume something to appease their negative view of themselves.", concludes Leonardo.

— So, Mr. Leonardo, please understand. At the end of it all, feeling useful is the most important element that must be in complete harmony so that the person can feel happy. And do you know why all this about happiness is so important? People also want to do what they like and gives them pleasure. Something that really helps them feel accomplished. It is like us hamsters. If we are unhappy or stressed, we chatter our teeth. — says Filomena, highlighting her primordial behavior.

— That is why professionals who achieve this are known as professionally accomplished, and there is one more element to be included in the list: the company must have and demonstrate the concern to know whether people are really happy with the work they do. And that this is done in an authentic and legitimate way. — continues Leonardo in his reflection.

— But you didn't answer my question, Leo. What are you afraid of? What do you think of your performance here at the company? What bothers you? Are you happy? — Filomena resumes, not letting Leonardo deviate from the subject.

— Filomena, these are important questions that I ask myself all the time: what should people really look for in their perspectives? Do they want more responsibilities, better access to information, gain more autonomy, have a status that gives visibility and the ability to make decisions, to take on a vice-presidency role, be part of an important Board of Directors, achieve the effective improvement of their professional role, take the leadership of a technical team? This bothers me, because I don't know the answer. I don't think anyone knows! — answers Leonardo.

"I see that there are many possibilities and many variables involved, but the thinking that emerges is: should all the organizational effort to make people happier be concentrated on allowing each person to actually recreate their professional role as so that the person can become more and more capable of making their potential be revealed and put at the service of their happiness as a professional?", asks Leonardo.

"I think that my performance here in the company must go through this. Allow my colleagues to see this, realize this and..." — vented Leonardo, when he is interrupted by Filomena.

— But Leo, do you think the company can demonstrate that it has real concern about these issues in relation to people? At home I feel that there is a real concern from your mother and you that I am well and happy. From you to her, ensuring that she is always well and happy, and from her to you, in the same way. — highlights Filomena.

— I realize that my colleagues, and I include myself, are unable to truly feel, perceive and believe that there is a legitimate concern for our well-being at work. What we see is something fake. It is utilitarian. — vented Leonardo. — I agree with you, Filomena. Sometimes I feel that it is necessary to do something very different to try to awaken in people that there is much more than the exchange in money, responsibility and power. The essence of each person, what they really feel good about being able to help others, whether they are colleagues, customers or suppliers. If there is something that makes me a little scared, it is that, that I am not able to make people develop this perception. — confesses Leonardo, visibly distressed.

— But, Leo. There is a big trap here. We hamsters, for example, until we learn to trust our owner, are left with a high level of stress. Then, if we trust too much, we start to think that all the space we can access is ours and we gnaw, gnaw, gnaw, messing up everything. Most people don't like this at all, you know? So, Leonardo, it seems to me that it's a question of balance! — teaches Filomena.

— Yes, Filomena, have you ever thought what it would be like if everyone's vocation really worked as the epicenter of their happiness? This would radiate to all those who relate to you and at that moment your vocation towards work would become uncertain. When this happened, things would become difficult for the professional, as he would possibly need to make the decision to abandon his conventional career, based on meritocratic conquests and replace them with a protean career, that is, based on the person's effective discoveries related to their vocation. Only then the professional could go in search of real happiness. — taught Leonardo, who is also well versed in subjects related to cognitive dissonance.

↑

Leonardo's mind is really bright and restless. He keeps searching every second for a way of thinking that is different from everything he had ever thought, always looking at the many possibilities that are related. Holistic view is the name of this. To look at a scenario and interpret it as a whole without losing sight of every detail that makes it up. By creating his alter ego and still projecting it as an escape valve in a primordial being, the hamster Filomena, he manages to police himself and use this metaphor of the hamster world to remind himself and his colleagues, that things in the day to day at work can be much simpler than they might realize. It is a great opportunity. Leonardo is not intimidated by the way people see what he thinks or how he thinks. He simply goes ahead believing in the transformation that his actions can promote.

Chapter 9 - The meeting

It was time to go to the General Director's Office.

Leonardo was concerned about Filomena.

"What will be waiting for me there? What kind of alignment will take place? Will I be suspended or summarily fired due to the non-conformities I caused here in my department?", thought Leonardo, worried about the call he received.

— Lucy did Miss Stella say anything else when she asked me to go to the General Director's Office? — asked Leonardo reluctantly.

— She told me that you were expected there in twenty minutes for an alignment meeting with the General Director and curiously asked that you take Filomena with you. — said Lucy.

— And nothing else? — insisted Leonardo.

Lucy looked at Leonardo and realized that he was feeling insecure. As much as she tried to reassure him by saying that Miss Stella's tone was friendly and light, she knew that Leonardo had crossed the line that separates the trenches of trickery and logic. She is also aware that she is a direct accomplice to this. Not that she wasn't worried enough. She was! But she also knew that if something very severe was imminent, she would have noticed some other movement coming from the General Director and it certainly would not be just a meeting with a specific time set.

— No, nothing more. — replied Lucy. — Why, Leonardo? Do you think you may have a problem? It is true that things here are very agitated and a bit messy too, right? — completed Lucy. — You don't think we should soften the uproar caused so far, at least by organizing the things you brought a little better?

— It's true, Lucy. It's really messy. But let me tell you: that is the intention! To disturb! Without all this movement with people being curious, uncomfortable and even a little insecure, I will not be able to achieve my goal of transforming the way we see things and think beyond the obvious. Please leave everything exactly as it is. There are a lot of things scattered around, I know. But help me with this, please? Let's keep it that way. — asked Leonardo, showing a little more determination.

— Of course, Leonardo. Don't worry! I'll leave everything as it is. I'll see that no one changes anything. — Lucy replied solicitously.

— Yes, Lucy. Please. Do that. The first thing for the transformation to start taking place is that people realize that nothing is ever ready; simply because we want them to be; just because we said they are; just because we organize our desks or because we followed the processes to the letter. They need to realize that the real transformation is just having the feeling that, in fact, nothing is ever ready, but in a continuous process of accommodation. — oriented Leonardo.

Renewed, Leonardo goes to Filomena's Work Station and picks her up from the exercise wheel, puts her in the bottom of the right pocket of his jacket and goes to the main elevator to go to the twentieth floor, to his General Director's office, Teressa.

Leonardo is not bothered at all by the live streaming that some colleagues continue to do, he is very calm and acts naturally as if he were immersed in a kind of real life movie, in real time, and in which smartphone cameras are ignored by him and his attitudes and movements are natural, normal, even prosaic. #FilomenaIsGoingForAWalk

As we know, the mind is fantastic and can cover in a minute a whole range of possibilities, playing like a film, very accelerated by the mind.

In the case of Leonardo, with his brilliant way of thinking and seeing the world, this is enhanced...

Chapter 10 - The identity

Leonardo has a big doubt on his mind.

As he goes to the elevator he reflects... carefully puts his hand in the bottom of the right pocket of his jacket and gently touches Filomena... when he touches her he feels that her pulse is slightly accelerated, practically vibrating at about five hundred beats per minute.

Hamsters love to stay in the comfort of dark spaces, after all in nature they create deep burrows and with several chambers. The problem is that the smell on Leonardo's clothes bothers her, leaving her a little agitated. He knows this, but his pocket is the safest place for her to stay while he travels the company's corridors.

— Leonardo, every time I go to your pocket, I have to cover my little nose, which as you know is very sensitive. That smell of fabric softener bothers me, you know? Well, I told you that today! Please at least put a handkerchief here to minimize it a little! Can you do that? — asks Filomena with a sarcastic delicacy.

— I'm doing it right now, Filomena. I'm going to go to the bathroom and get some really soft paper towels to put here for you. Is that okay for you? — thought Leonardo to minimize Filomena's discomfort.

— Great, thank you for your attention! — replied Filomena as Leonardo dodged the elevator heading towards the bathroom where he took some sheets of paper towel and lined the right pocket of his jacket, making a better space for Filomena.

— That's it, Leonardo! That's a lot better! — praised Filomena with relief.

— So, Filomena. You know that I have been thinking about the question of the balance of interests between the organization and the professionals being really an exchange of mutual concessions, which will only be effectively functional if they can satisfy both sides. In other words, people need to "carry on with their lives" so that it gives real meaning to the things they do. Do you see any sense in this? — asked Leonardo.

— Leonardo, I am a primordial being, so it is very simple and, from my perspective, what you said makes perfect sense. For us, hamsters, if we are in the wild, we try to protect ourselves from predators in our dens, rest a lot during the day to go out at night in search of food that we accumulate in our elastic little cheeks. So we always have a little reserve of food, in case we can't go out and look for more or if food will be scarce for some reason. — teaches Filomena.

— Furthermore, we always seek, of course, to reproduce, after all our life expectancy is three and a half years on average. When we are in the condition of pets, our main concern is to stay in shape so that we don't die of boredom, as we are naturally agitated. We still need to always have something available to nibble or our teeth will become giant and lastly, of course, we need to eat. And no, we are not greedy, we only eat what we need to eat and nothing else. So, this 'carrying on with their lives', for us it has this meaning, survival in balance. — replied Filomena, calmly and wisely.

— I wonder, Filomena, if my colleagues had the maturity and the opportunity so that they could recreate their own work environment, freely, without worrying too much about the consequences of it, but focused only on doing their best in the best way possible. I think it could be magical. — ponders Leonardo, dreaming of his colleagues going to another stage of human consciousness and self-realization with work.

— That's right, Leonardo. I have understood almost everything. What do you mean by recreating your own work environment? — provokes Filomena. — Because for us hamsters, it would not make much sense for me to want to recreate something that is working. For example, I want to be more than my eventual den mate. It is enough that whoever is in the same hole that I have the same objective, that is, to carry their life. Except for here, in the artificial environment you created for me, my Workstation. In this case, what I really want is a series of improvements, which I have already asked you for... — explains Filomena.

— Okay, Filomena, I will work on the improvements of your Workstation. But coming back, for us humans, this recreating would be something like working in a renowned company; having co-workers who are happy too; earning a good salary; doing the things you like ... that's what my colleagues understand about recreating and being happy with their work, but in fact, it's not that simple, Filomena. I see it differently. The happiness of working in a company is composed of a set of elements that constitute not only what the company is and represents in the market as its brand, its products, its tradition of quality, but fundamentally what is the identity of the people who are there. Yes, after all, the company is essentially made up of people who, if they are truly happy, will probably work better. And my understanding of being happy goes far beyond the items mentioned above, which, in my view, are utilitarian. It is about achieving a balance between all the components that participate in and make up the organizational ecosystem. — explains Leonardo, defending his dream and his desire.

— I know, Leonardo. It may even be all that you just said. However, in my view, much simpler, more primordial, it makes no sense, for example, to look for a better owner. Especially because we can't do that. What we try to do is to have the best life we can with what is given to us by our owners. If we are not comfortable or if we are unhappy, the most we can do is to be stressed and chatter our teeth. So, for us, to recreate, it will be at most to chew some hamster bedding to soften our walk, and to be happy is to be well fed and exercise daily. — explains Filomena with all simplicity. — Of course, if this is taken to our natural environment, then things change, because if the burrow we dig, in nature, it's not a good location, if it is very difficult to find food in that place or if there are many predators that really threaten us, so in that case, we're going to move. We will dig another hole in another place where conditions are better and more favorable. — explains Filomena simply.

— In that sense, Filomena, we humans share a very interesting parallel here. The companies are constituted by a structural body that are their buildings, furniture, machines, equipment, vehicles, furniture, that is, all the physical part, not human.

They are also made of another structuring part that are the systems, processes, methods, functional methodologies, that is, its organizational intelligence. And lastly, a living part, human in this case, that uses the structuring part to make the processes operate within the structural body and in this way effectively make things happen in different organizational contexts. — teaches Leonardo, drawing on the concept of classical administration, a subject in which he is versed. — This also happens with your Workstation and accessories that are the physical part, the instinctive use that you make of the spaces are like the structuring part and you, in this case, are the living part that uses all this. — complements Leonardo in his reasoning.

— However, when you are in nature, you are the owner of your space, your burrow. And you keep it, take care of it your way. If it's not a good place, you move and that's it! Here, for humans, this would be the equivalent of what we call being the owner of the business or entrepreneur. When this is the case, the control that people have over what they do, how they do it and why they do it is much greater. Although in the first case, people can also move and work in another company. Unlike you, which when kept as pets, can't change owners. — reflects Leonardo, comparing scenarios in his mind.

* ↑ *

In the elevator access lounge, Leonardo watches his colleagues talking to each other about Filomena's habitat, her Workstation in the office. Some more discreet ones just look at Leonardo and make an expression of normality. Others nod their heads discreetly in a kind of sneaky greeting. Others still look at Leonardo with suspicion, as if he posed a threat to organizational order and security.

It is always difficult to face the challenge of being and doing differently in the quest to transform people. Everyone is suspicious and this is natural, as these attitudes mortally injure the comfort zone that each one has built for themselves and within which they have settled in to feel safe.

In fact, Leonardo is not bothered by the distrust generated. He just feels that he is in a kind of crusade which is understood by some as a failed attempt to transform something that is crystallized in people's heads, while others understand it as a possibility to transform people, but they feel hostage to the organization thinking that it won't allow the transformation to take place.

Upon reaching the elevator, Leonardo touches the panel and waits for it, but his mind does not stop.

The possibilities are many and his mascot, Filomena, inspires him... constantly.

↓

— Well, Leonardo. If I have a choice, I don't want to change owners. You are good to me! Your mother is very good to me! You take care of me, feed me, give me a little house that is really cool and care about me. I don't want to change owners and I don't want to go to nature. — says Filomena in Leonardo's mind.

— Thank you, Filomena. I feel the same way. I don't want to let someone else take care of you, let alone return you to nature. You are my pet and at home you are our starlet, mine and my mother's. — reflects Leonardo, feeling the vibration of Filomena's Heart reduce, now that it has soft paper towel minimizing the smell in the pocket of his jacket.

↑

The elevator arrives. Leonardo enters and asks for the 20th floor: General Director's Office. Starting from the eighth floor, where the Marketing and Products Department managed by Leonardo is located, there will only be twelve floors, but in his mind a lot happens. Leonardo's mind is fantastic.

↓

— Filomena, you know that in an organization all parties are interdependent, that is, they depend on each other so that, in a structured and harmonious way, they collaborate to deliver the value that the company offers, that is, to function well! All of these elements, when brought together, form the organizational ecosystem. As such, they constitute an entity, therefore alive, pulsating and at the same time dependent on a delicate balance to maintain itself well. That is how it manages to guarantee the smooth functioning of all its parts. — considers Leonardo.

— As much as common sense may unfortunately lead people to think that companies are made up only of buildings, machines, equipment and processes, they forget who makes it all work. People do it. As much as automation is increasingly present in the daily lives of organizations, it is people who really make things happen. — Leonardo speaks, reaffirming and coming to the conclusion that he could not give up his endeavor, after all, he put his reputation at stake with his decisions and attitudes.

— Leonardo, listen. I'll try to help you here! I will use my most basic way of looking at things. The most primordial I can. Okay... So that our hamster happiness can be built, so that it really settles down, it depends first and foremost on the feeling of security being present in the environment where we live. This sense of security includes simple elements that we inherit from nature. So, for example, there is no point in having an organized, beautiful, safe, full of cameras, cozy and dry place and with enough food available, if there is no possibility of finding a mate to reproduce. Why? Because reproducing is part of our nature and there will come a time when we will be at such a high level of stress for not having this company, that we simply hibernate and never return... then we die! — says Filomena, nudging Leonardo, practically asking for a companion.

— That's it! For this truth about happiness to be understood and incorporated by my colleagues, it must be an achievement. They need to be sure that the decisions they make will not be judged but understood as doing their best. Until this happens, it will be impossible to start preparing them, and that includes my General Director. Everyone needs to understand that they can choose the best way to act in the company of which they are a part of. And they need to learn how to share this. — concludes Leonardo, confident and happy. — Using the metaphor of the hamster world, it is possible to implement the mindset through the perspective of Filomena.

First, it will be necessary to ensure the balance of interdependencies. For example, her Workstation is not perfect, the way she would like it, but it serves the purpose well and I will make the promised improvements. As long as the promised improvements do not arrive, it is necessary to be careful and zealous so that everything on her Workstation is working well: that there is no shortage of seeds, that everything is always clean and that the spaces for her to exercise are always working. Last but not least, there is learning. Filomena is small, fragile and totally dependent on me. If I forget about Filomena she will die. On the other hand, if she doesn't behave well, I'll be upset. All of this is quite complex. The more our relationship matures, the more we will learn from each other and the better our coexistence will be, since we will have an increase in mutual trust. If these elements of balance and trust are lost or become disordered, they can generate chaos that will lead to the collapse of that balance and the death of Filomena. — elaborates Leonardo, his approach to creating an understanding of true happiness with his colleagues, using the hamster metaphor for that.

— I understand, Filomena. My biggest challenge will be to work with my General Director, Teressa. I need her to understand and start to benefit from the knowledge of those same truths. With this, she will be able to plan management actions that improve the process of building the essential corporate identity to achieve success and results, developing an effectively happy team. — concluded Leonardo, much more confident now.

— Ah, Filomena. When I speak to you, adjectives like innocence, purity and even naivety come to mind. — reflects Leonardo, stroking Filomena's head. — These elements seem to have no time or even a voice within the organizational context where I live today. It is as if I myself were a hamster that is unhappy with its owner and wants to chatter teeth to signal that things are not looking good. In fact, that's what I'm doing! The achievement of happiness may even be one of the motivators for my colleagues, but in order for them to achieve this, they will have to combine a very large number of elements which, perhaps, they do not understand very well at this initial moment. Bringing you here is the opportunity to cause a huge shock in the potential and thus try to bring out innocence, purity and ingenuity in people. This is a good idea! — thought Leonardo, even more confident.

↑

— 20th floor. — informed the melodic digital voice.

The elevator door opens, and Leonardo comes out with little Filomena in the right pocket of his jacket. He's much less anxious now. The reflections gave him greater confidence. The digital clock on the

General Director's waiting room wall reads 11:06 am and the only person there is Miss Stella, the Executive Assistant to the General Director, Teressa.

Chapter 11 - Corporate scaffold

— Hello again, Leonardo. — said Miss Stella, quietly.

— Hello... hey, Stella! Where is everyone? Does Teressa have any meetings in progress? — Leonardo is astonished by the unusually empty waiting room.

— She asked me to cancel the meetings this morning, Leonardo. It seems that you two need to align on some topics and she didn't want to be distracted. I'll let her know that you've arrived. — said Miss Stella with serenity. She was already picking up the phone when...

— Please, Miss Stella. Wait just a minute! Do you know why Teressa called me here? — asked Leonardo, showing some apprehension.

— Come on, Leonardo. What do you think? This morning's events on the eighth floor gained notoriety. They spread throughout our company and even over the Internet. Your initiative was able to highlight you, our company and Filomena, as targets of various memes. Even live broadcasts were and are still going. Not to mention the hashtags #MyManagerHasGoneCrazy, #CoolOffice, #TheAmazingFilomena and #NewToy. When Teressa saw everything that was happening, she almost had an attack. Fortunately, I managed to calm her spirits, or you would leave that room straight out of the company or worse... — said Miss Stella, harshly.

— That's right! I understand. — replied Leonardo a little ashamed, but at the same time firmly.

— And before I forget... — replied Miss Stella. — Who is this Filomena? — she asked curiously.

Leonardo carefully put his hand in the right pocket of his jacket and from there, with affection, removed the small, fragile and docile Filomena.

In the palm of Leonardo's hand, little Filomena scratches her pink nose and looks at Miss Stella with all the innocence of her tiny black eyes.

The expression on Miss Stella's face lights up with joy and tenderness when she sees that little animal so comfortable in Leonardo's hands. Calm, docile, sweet, cute and simple.

— She is beautiful... how cute! Loved it! Can I pet her? — asked Miss Stella, very delighted with little Filomena.

— Not yet, Miss Stella. Filomena is very sensitive and can be stressed by changing hands or being touched by a stranger. It is better that she stays with me. She is very special. She's my beautiful starlet. —

said Leonardo as he stroked Filomena's head, excited that she had immediately won over Miss Stella.

— Ah, such a cutie... I wanted to pet her so much ... — Miss Stella insists.

— Everything in its time, Miss Stella. Okay? In its time! — says Leonardo.

— That's right! I'll let Teressa know. — said Miss Stella with a face of tenderness as she called, clearly won over by the primordial simplicity of the tiny animal.

— Yes... okay, I'll let him know... thanks! You can go in now, Leonardo. — said Miss Stella, without taking her eyes off Filomena, who Leonardo carefully put back in the right pocket of his jacket.

↓

— Wow, Leonardo. Miss Stella got pretty charmed, huh? I thought she was going to take me from your hand by force. I was even a little scared, you know? — observed Filomena.

— Don't worry, Filomena, I won't let anyone grab you without you wanting to, okay? — reflected Leonardo.

— You better! And this Teressa? Can I trust her? — Filomena said.

— Yes, Filomena. You can!

— But isn't that the one who escorted you out of her office earlier today?

— Yes, Filomena, she did it!

— So... and you still say she is trustworthy...

— Yes, Filomena. She is!

— Okay, then! If you are saying...

↑

— Hello, excuse me! Did you send for me, Teressa? — said Leonardo, as he entered the General Director's office.

— Leonardo, Leonardo... you are really naughty... you know how to shake things up. Please sit down. Make yourself comfortable. — Teressa said warmly as she walked towards the coffee counter. — Would you like a drink, Leonardo? A tea? Coffee? — she asked, elegantly.

— Yes, please. Coffee! — replied Leonardo, sitting down.

— Sugar or sweetener, Leonardo?

— Neither, please!

— Wise decision. Pure coffee is the best. That's the only way one can smell and taste the true aroma and flavor. I still can't, you know? I need to add a drop of stevia or two to make it taste good.

— I liked it with sugar, Teressa, but I met a barista at that new coffee shop that opened last year next to the Pittoresque Restaurant. He taught me to enjoy coffee without additives.

— Oh, I know ... the Toasted Grain Coffee Shop?

— Yes, Toasted Grain. It's great over there. And there are some delicious treats too.

— Ah Leonardo, I confess that I like to go there for them. That pistachio pie they make... I love it! And the baked snacks then... delicious!

— I love macaron. I always eat at least three different colors. With pure coffee it is a perfect combination.

Teressa is a mature woman in her forties. An indomitable single, she lives for work and for her vacation trips with her girlfriends. She loves to travel, especially sea cruises. She has always worked in the management area in which he graduated and specialized, emphasizing in product development and in multidisciplinary teams. She has been with the company for more than twenty years and has passed through practically all management chairs until she reached the General Directorate. Teressa is also a teacher in the art of treading calmly and later asserting her points of view. She finds in Miss Stella her balance when making decisions. It is the person who always brings her the arguments, counterarguments, and the reflections for her to make the best decisions.

Leonardo was getting relaxed with Teressa's friendly attitude. He sat in the comfortable chair in front of her table while coffee was served. He observed that she was very calm and tried to make him also calm and at ease. Very different from what happened earlier when he went there to present his initiative.

— Leonardo, I asked you to come here so that we could discuss a little better what you brought me to suggest earlier and to evaluate the developments of what you ended up doing despite of what we talked about. I clearly remember, Leonardo, telling you not to proceed with your initiative, but that is not what happened. You went back to your department and proceeded with the assembly of that Playful Space that you had told me about. I was quite busy when you came in earlier today and I couldn't explain the details of why we might not be able to move forward with your idea at this point, so now I need to bring up some considerations. — said Teressa, who paused to sip coffee.

Leonardo also sipped and listened carefully to Teressa's comments, which proceeded in a calm and linear manner.

— You told me that the area occupied by the Playful Space would be approximately 21 square feet, that is, about 4.5ft. x 4.5ft. The standard size of our circulation aisles is 5 ft., so the circulation space would be obstructed. Another factor is that a Playful Space in the middle of the corridor will be a distraction for the staff and I confess to you that I couldn't see a practical sense in all of this. You also told me that this playful space would be inhabited by a pet. And if that wasn't enough, you thought and decided to do everything without even discussing with me. Do you agree that I have every reason to be very disappointed with your actions, Leonardo? — Teressa said pointedly, but calmly, while taking another sip of coffee.

— True, Teressa. I ended up crossing the line that separates logic and trickery in opposite trenches. With no harm to my intentions, which are sure to be the best ones, I took a chance to demonstrate something that otherwise would not be possible.

— But Leonardo, are you aware of how many infractions you committed with your actions this morning?

— Yes, I am! There were at least seven, eight if you consider insubordination to your direct determination.

— So, Leonardo! You and your department jumped from 1st place in operational compliance to 1st place in non-compliance in just one morning of work. Congratulations! Put yourself in my place now and answer me: would you continue to trust you after your attitude? Be honest with me!

— Well, Teressa. I would have a hard time trusting, but I would give myself the benefit of the doubt[27]. At least I would listen very carefully to the intentions that motivated my attitudes, and then, only after that, decide something.

— I understand the same way, Leonardo. That's why I called you here and cancelled the rest of this morning's schedule, just so you can explain carefully what the intentions are. If you allow me, I will call Miss Stella to accompany us. All right?

— Sure, Teressa, I think it's great.

Picking up the phone, Teressa asked Miss Stella to join her and Leonardo at the meeting. While Leonardo sipped some more coffee, Teressa checked if there was any notification on her smartphone.

— Excuse me...

— Please, Miss Stella. Join us. I gave Leonardo a brief review of the events that I noticed since this morning regarding the initiative he decided to undertake here at the company. I asked him to share his intentions in a more detailed way, so that starting from this understanding we can deliberate the next steps, whatever they may be. Leonardo, can you please give us the details of what you really intend to do?

"Oh my... I don't know if I'll be able to remember exactly the sequence I thought to convey my idea, but I'll do my best, after all it seems that my future here at the company will depend a lot on what I'm going to say right now.", reflected Leonardo with a little worry.

— Leonardo... Leo... LEO... — called Filomena whispering.

— What is it Filomena, can't you see that I'm busy now? What do you want?

— Leo, look ... you need to keep it simple. Don't to explain too much, justify too much, illustrate too much... go for the simplest way and everything will be all right, okay? — oriented Filomena.

— Fine. I will do this, but there are some things that I need to put in context, or my arguments will be weak.

— Right but be objective. Deal?

— Deal, Filomena!

↑

Leonardo was mentally preparing to begin his explanation. He saw Miss Stella sit down and the General Director, Teressa, sit in her comfortable chair. He put his hand in the right pocket of his jacket and touched Filomena gently. He could feel her peace with that little heart vibrating quietly. He took his hand out of his pocket, took a breath, and began his explanation.

— About a year ago, just before I went on vacation, after we finished the launch of that new product for single men, the Alfa Guide, which proved to be a success, I was quite stressed because I didn't see that we had achieved effectively a new product. All we managed to do was create a small variation of a product that we had already removed from the catalog a few years ago. That made me very sad. — Leonardo started by pulling his colleagues' reasoning and remembering a bit of the history of the Marketing and Products department.

— After the first sales results came out, I gathered my team and went through the results with them. What I realized from the team was that their view of the concept of success is very limited. For them, the fact that we had a demand in orders greater than our best mark of the previous year by about 15% was enough to label the product as being successful.

But I didn't see it that way. — Leonardo brought his vision more as a Marketing Manager.

— Analyzing the market as a whole at the time, competition, similar products in the market, imports and promotions, I concluded that if the product had really been an innovative proposal, we would have had the potential to advance our best previous index by more than 30%, and not just 15%. But, in fact, that wasn't what bothered me the most, it was the fact that my team was content with that limiting concept of success. — explained Leonardo.

— I don't remember you sharing this perception with us, Leonardo! – Miss Stella said, and Teressa showed agreement.

— Yes, it's true I did not share it, because I knew that as the Marketing and Products Manager, I was responsible for changing this situation in my team and as I was about to go on vacation, I postponed the addressing of this issue after my return. — Leonardo justified.

— During my vacation I took a short five-day trip with my mother to my grandparents' house in the countryside and upon my return I dedicated the other ten days to do something unlike anything I had done so far in terms of hobby. I decided to research the creation of dioramas.

— Dioramas? What is this, Leonardo? — asked Teressa.

— It is an art form in which you build a kind of model, a miniature representation of the real world, but that goes further, as it requires dynamic realism, movement and the essence of emotion. The challenge is to give movement and emotion to a scene that will be represented in a static way. It is very common to see dioramas with scenes from famous battles, nature scenes, prosaic urban scenes, movie scenes and so on. — explained, Leonardo.

— When I started assembling my first diorama, I chose to represent the environment of this company, specifically the movement that I perceived to have in my department. With all people interacting, happy about the results, happy for their colleagues being happy, feeling really fulfilled. I made the action figures, the dolls, which would be the bases for the characters in the diorama, the furniture, the area we have for our coffee there on the eighth floor, the work stations, I set everything up and after I finished I did the exercise of contemplation. Do you know what I saw?

— Is this a rhetorical question, Leonardo, or do you expect us to guess? — asked Miss Stella.

— Take your best shot ...

— I don't know, you saw that as it was your first diorama, it was poorly done, and you would need to start all over again and practice the technique more... — replied Miss Stella.

— And you, Teressa. What do you think I saw?

— I have no idea, Leonardo... I don't know... something was missing?

— Miss Stella, in the case of the technique, at the time, I still needed to refine it a little, but the representation of the space was, even in my first diorama, quite faithful to our space on the eighth floor, with all the details of painting, decoration, workstations, lighting, people, interactions, access routes and exits, and everything else. And yes, Teressa, I saw that something very important was missing in my diorama: vitality, vibration and energy. Have I not been able to meet the most difficult challenge of a diorama? I thought about it! I was intrigued by that, because although my technique still needs to be improved, it was already quite realistic, visually speaking. — Leonardo explained and continued.

— So, I decided to challenge myself with another scene. A natural landscape, this time. I picked a scene from one of those wildlife documentaries and chose one in which two lions compete in the African savanna for the alpha male position in their pack. The fight was violent. Each animal was about 8 feet long and about 400 pounds. Its roars made the cameraman shiver and while the fight was taking place, the rest of the pack, females and a few cubs of varying ages, gathered in a relatively close corner in the savanna, awaiting the outcome of the fight. — Leonardo explained, moved.

— After a few days, when I finished this second diorama, I went to contemplate it for a while. Do you know what I found out? That although my technique in the construction of this diorama did not improve significantly compared to the first one about the office, the fidelity of the scene was just as good as it, and I noticed that the vitality, vibration and energy that a diorama needs were present. I looked at and contemplated the scene of the fight between those two beasts from all angles, with all the different lights and nuances and it was there... vibrant emotion. — narrates with emotion Leonardo, continuing.

— I discovered then that the scene I made of the office, despite being my first diorama, was as realistic as the second one I built. So, the problem was not with my technique of making dioramas with vitality, vibration and that transmit energy in the scene portrayed. The problem was really what I portrayed. My department was what had low vitality, almost no vibration and very low energy. — concluded Leonardo in his initial explanation, when he was questioned by Teressa.

— And after that, Leonardo? When you came back from vacation, what did you do?

— On my return from vacation, with this observation in my mind, I was very concerned with finding a way to revert this situation and I began to observe more carefully the daily lives of people in the office, the behavior of colleagues on the eighth floor. It became clear to me, day after day, project after project, challenge after challenge, that each and all of them, and I include myself in that, were operating the company's processes in an exemplary manner, doing what was expected to be done by the department, but without that desire for creation and innovation that each new product must have. What's the consequence of this? Everyone stopped getting happiness from the work that everyone there likes to do, that is, thinking about products that are magical for the people who use them. I started to observe a downward spiral of success in our products. And you have seen for yourself, Teressa, our best result in new products was no more than a 15% increase, when in previous years we reached 35% easily, and in some we reached 40%. — explains, Leonardo, sadly.

— And when was that exactly, your finding about your team, Leonardo? — asked Miss Stella.

— About eight months ago I started the observation and I have noticed it's proving to be increasingly severe in my department.

— Right, Leonardo. Interesting! And how does this new initiative of yours fit into all of this? — asked Teressa, still not understanding his attitudes.

— Well, after I noticed this lack of happiness in my team, I started making some small movements, looking for ways I could generate engagement and recovery of everyone's happiness. My first attempt was to invite my colleagues for a hike in nature, through a trail in the forest, a guided tour with contemplation, swimming in a waterfall, and transportation provided. I did this without the company. It was a kind of action between coworkers. Of the 38 employees I have there in my department, 30 joined, but only 12 went for the hike. It was a very good, fun and highly engaging experience for those who participated. That injected an important mood boost, but the low adhesion was already a clue that this would not be the way forward. Also, because those who didn't attend felt displaced afterwards around the conversations exchanged by those who participated. The activity caused the formation of a type of "hiking people group" versus the "non-hiking people group". I worked hard to minimize that later. — and Leonardo continued.

— My second attempt was a celebration event for the closing of the Alfa Guide results with an increase of 15% in the quarter. In this initiative, I used my budget as Department Manager for corporate events that I approved with the Human Resources Department. I also got some gifts from suppliers to use as giveaways, we had barbecue, karaoke, and kart racing. It was very good! We had a wonderful day. Altogether there were 37 coworkers. Only Leila, who was on maternity leave, could not go. As a result, I noticed that the team's interaction and mood showed a general improvement in the three weeks following the event, then it decreased until it returned to the level it was before the event. — Leonardo narrated carefully.

Teressa and Miss Stella were eager to understand how far Leonardo wanted to go with his narrative, which would lead up to the events of that day. Despite their anxiety, they were also really willing to understand the whole context. One thing was clear to them, that Leonardo was looking for a way to reverse a scenario with his team that only he was realizing and that if reversed would mean a turnaround in the company's results, once again.

— My third attempt was one that caused confusion because of the company's civil liability in relation to events offered to its employees for training purposes.

— Ah, that was the challenge in the rapids, the rafting, and the balloon ride. — recalled Miss Stella.

— You're right, Miss Stella. There was total adhesion. Even Leila who had just returned from her maternity leave decided to go. At this event, I realized that all colleagues achieved great synergy and integration. I think that realizing the interdependencies in rafting and then the complicity in ballooning were decisive. I felt the team more integrated and happy for about five weeks, I was even starting to get excited about the strategy. But, again, I saw that things had not managed to be sustained, as it didn't reach the essence I was looking for in the vitality, vibration and energy needed in my department. — shared Leonardo with them.

— So, two months ago I was at the Farmer's Market with my mother looking for some seeds for our vegetable and flower gardens at home, when I passed by one of these pet shops. I confess to you that I never liked having pets. Neither cat nor dog. My mom always liked it. We have Boris, a pug dog. At most I had an aquarium once, a long time ago. I was still a teenager. Well, the goldfish committed suicide. Poor guy, he jumped out of the tank! I was traumatized at the time. My mother offered us to buy another one and I found it very depressing. Then I came to know that some fish tend to do that, so you need to have a lid on the tank. But anyway. I didn't want to know about having a pet anymore. But what caught my attention at the pet shop was a colorful habitat that was sold in modules for use with hamsters. I went into the store, asked the salesman some questions, which left me delighted with the possibilities. Combining this with the techniques I developed to build dioramas, I felt like the Greek Archimedes himself and shouted: Eureka!

— And what was your discovery, Leonardo? — asked Teressa and Miss Stella almost together.

— Well, so that I could motivate my team, I first needed to generate a situation of awkwardness, with something totally unusual, that would really be in their way, but that at the same time that it would create engagement in some, the excess of zeal in others, because while some people like cute little pets, others don't like animals, no matter how cute they are. Second, it would need to offer something playful in the habitat so that at the same time that it generates attraction or aversion, depending on the taste of each person, it would still stimulate their imagination. This is why I created an Interactive Play Space, because with it we have an interesting scenario, reminiscent of a diorama, representing the style of a hamster's habitat, but very colorful and fun to observe with spaces that resemble our own human lifestyle. And lastly, we have all the matters related to hamster care. A nice, peaceful and primordial little animal that is a lot of fun. — Leonardo explains, leaving Miss Stella and Teressa motivated with his narrative.

↓

— Hey... hey... Leo... won't you be introducing me to Teressa? Because I already met Miss Stella. — called Filomena, whispering.

— Sure, wait just a little bit, it's going to be now. Make your most beautiful and cute face, okay?

— Leo, look... you know I'm always cute, that's how I am, just cute and beautiful.

↑

— So Teressa, that was how I met Filomena and all the possibilities that this primordial little being can teach us with its simplicity. — said Leonardo as he lovingly put his hand in the right pocket of his jacket and carefully removed Filomena from there.

With a light, smooth movement, Leonardo brought the little hamster into the palm of his hand. Its coffee and milk colored coat, with her shiny little hairs that reflected the natural light that came through the large glass window of the room on the twentieth floor. Beautiful! Its prominent whiskers moved around looking for the safe support of Leonardo's hands. Her little black eyes and pink nose were charming. She sat in Leonardo's hand, put her front paws together and stood there, quietly, staring at Teressa and Miss Stella. Miss Stella's reaction was tender when she saw Filomena's grace once more in that pose of a true starlet. Teressa's reaction was ...

— Leonardo, so this is Filomena! I see why everyone wanted to meet this little girl. She is gorgeous... so sweet, so docile, so cute... can I hold her in my hand? — asked Teressa ...

— I don't recommend it, Teressa. Filomena is a little stressed today... I only brought her here at your request. She was already in the gym when you called me and I pulled her out of her morning aerobics. She gets stressed when I interrupt her exercise. — said Leonardo.

— Does she have an exercise room? — asked Teressa, surprised.

— Yes, and a lot more. The Playful and Interactive Space, in fact Filomena's Workstation is a complete house. — replied Leonardo excitedly.

— But she is so cute...

— Isn't she?

— I love it.

Miss Stella and Teressa were in love with the little hamster Filomena. Leonardo knew there was still a long way to go. For he had not yet revealed his whole plan to them. Some details were still missing. The most important ones, actually.

— Leonardo. Your attitude of stirring things up in your department was brilliant. I always thought that the Innovation teams of a company should be really bold and do things without fear of being happy. — Teressa spoke.

— It's true, Teressa. I agree with you on that point, but while I was preparing Filomena's Playful and Interactive Space, things got a little out of control, you know? I wanted to apologize for that! We are live on the Internet and there are a lot of memes exposing what I did this morning. I confess that I'm a little embarrassed! — Leonardo was speaking, carefully treading the situation and how he would talk through the next steps.

↓

— Shhh ... Leonardo. Is this woman crazy? When you came here in the morning to talk about what you intended to do, she almost kicked you out of her office! And now she's different, all solicitous and complimenting you. I don't understand! — whispered Filomena in Leonardo's mind.

— I'm also trying to understand, Filomena. Let's see which how this goes. — reflected Leonardo.

↑

— Well, my dear Leonardo. I finally understand what you are planning to do. Earlier today when you came to me, I was very upset that you didn't speak to me in advance about your initiative and I ended up not thinking properly about the possibilities. In fact, we now need to think together what the next steps should be. — said the Director, surprising Leonardo.

— Do you understand now, Teressa? Wow, good! What a relief! I thought I was in trouble! I am very happy that you have changed your mind about what I am trying to do. — said Leonardo.

— Of course, Leonardo. In fact, I think we have an excellent opportunity here. And I see no problem in reviewing my idea about your initiative, after all, only crazy people have a permanent idea, right? It's okay to change your position on something! — nudged Teressa.

— I loved Filomena! I loved to meet her. Well, she's a celebrity now. Essentially our official mascot. — said Teressa excitedly as she raised her hand towards Filomena with the intention of touching her, but stopped in the middle of her movement, just waving her fingertips, as if caressing her from a distance.

↓

— Calm down, Filomena. It's all right! I won't let anyone touch you. — thought Leonardo, whispering in his mind.

— Careful, huh! I don't want this crazy to touch me. — whispered Filomena.

↑

— Ah, but she is SO BEAUTIFUL AND CUTE!!! — shouted hysterically Teressa. — Much more beautiful than I thought. Can I hold it, can I? Please! — said Teressa, begging.

— It's better not, Teressa. Filomena is very sensitive. It may take a while for her to get used to people she doesn't know very well. She can get more stressed, you know? — Leonardo pondered calmly.

↓

— Please, Leonardo. Let me go back to your pocket. Please... — whispered Filomena.

— Of course, yes. Let's take it easy! — said Leonardo as he placed Filomena lovingly in the right pocket of his jacket.

↑

— Ah, putting her in your pocket already? — said Teressa, lamenting Filomena's absence.

— Yes! It's better that way. Before she gets stressed. — confirmed Leonardo.

— Okay, Leonardo, we don't want our beautiful Filomena stressed. — said the Director.

↓

— Wow? What is this story about 'ours'? Leonardo, please. I'm not someone else's, let alone this crazy woman. — whispered Filomena.

— It's just an expression, Filomena. Of course, you are not the company's, but mine and my mother's. — Leonardo reassured.

↑

— Good, Leonardo. What I want to agree with you is how we are going to announce this important change in our corporate environment with the insertion of Filomena in our space to promote the continuous development of our excellence seeking innovation. — mended Teressa.

— I also want to take advantage of this inspiration to create several disruptive environments and several decompression spaces with a strong playful theme. We will take care of everything so that your initiative is enhanced, Leonardo. — said the Director excited about all that.

— Right, Teressa. But can I share the rest of my vision first? — asked Leonardo.

— Please, Leonardo, go on! — said Teressa.

— Thank you! Well, to generate the awakening of happiness in our colleagues in my department, the first step I need to take is to make everyone feel safe and confident that the decisions made there, in our department, will not be reprimanded, but always received as the team's best achievement. — began, Leonardo.

— But isn't that already how it is, Leonardo? — asked Miss Stella.

— No, it's not! I realize that the team is totally restricted to our creative processes, respecting the sequence of work as if it was a cake recipe. As much as we have a small rework index, it does not mean that we are on the right path or on the best path, because we put the team in a cast. They are not innovating, they are just following premade recipes, with some minor variations. — explains Leonardo.

— So, you're proposing that we let them do whatever they want? Is that it? — asked Teressa.

— No, that's not it. What I am proposing is that they feel safe in taking risks, without fear of eventually reaping a result that is not the desired one. — explains Leonardo.

— And how does the Playful and Interactive Space and Filomena fit into this? — asked Miss Stella.

— I'll get there. Let me continue with the line of thought... so that my team realizes that our department has the flexibility to seek new creative possibilities, the first action is that this initiative of mine presented today is treated by the company as a totally normal event, that is, as much as all the buzz that has set in has generated this frenzy in the company and outside of it with memes, lives and hashtags, all of this was a confirmation that the transformation movement must start with the generation of initial discomfort before transformation happens. As everyone realizes that the company, in the figure of its General Director, treats this as a completely normal event, it will send the message that disruptive movements are normal and expected. This will give the initial safety we need everyone to feel. — explains Leonardo.

— Right, Leonardo. But how are we going to explain to the other departments of the company and to colleagues in their own departments that non-conformities are tolerable? We cannot make exceptions for committing non-conformities as if they were normal. — Teressa asks gravely.

— The control of non-conformities only serves to generate process compliance indicators. If our general process for certain conformities, such as the use of circulation space, is affected due to the need to generate stimuli for disruptive creation, then we need to adapt the process. — guides Leonardo and continues.

— If we need to guarantee the maintenance of interdependencies between the different departments of the company, but one of the departments require some adaptation, the speed in the adaptation to conformities of these interdependencies must be extremely fast and needs to come from the Board of Directors itself, making whatever adaptation is necessary so that it gives the safety that everyone needs to feel. That is, we need to adopt much more agile procedures for reviewing processes, or if we want to be really disruptive, we can eliminate some controls that are acting as barriers to the freedom that we need to have when working in a creative setting. — concludes Leonardo.

— But, Leonardo. Don't you fear that this will give everyone the feeling that the company does not care about following processes, allowing people to do everything their own way? — asked Miss Stella.

— On the contrary. It's one thing for our administrative and compliance processes that we need to follow as a result of our own business, it's another thing to establish that there is freedom for us to be creative and escape all of the plastered processes of creation and innovation. We need to send two very clear messages to everyone, starting with my department: first, that there is no innovation by decree. It only happens if people feel safe and happy with what they do, and; second, that the desired results will always be followed and sought the way they always were, but without the constraints of the creation process we have today. After all, creation is not following premade recipes, but creating recipes for every need that arises. — concludes Leonardo.

— And how do we do it then? — asked Teressa, curious.

— First, I need that the eight non-conformities that I committed today to be duly scored and immediately submitted to my department, directly to my Personal Assistant, Lucy, so that we can forward our suggestions and recommendations for the necessary adjustments. Then we will quickly make the necessary adjustments in the space so that everyone can participate in the inclusion of our starlet, Filomena, in our daily lives. This will generate at least two types of people: the first is the one that simply observes the Playful and Interactive Space and contemplates with the most diverse looks what is happening there; the second type will be the one that will really be involved, actually interacting, assuming responsibilities towards the Space and actively participating in its evolution, constant adaptation and improvement. — explains Leonardo.

— As these two types of public begin to form and interact naturally, they will have something in common, they will realize that the Playful and Interactive Space is here to stay and that the Board of Directors treated the novelty as something normal, as it made the necessary adaptations in our processes and norms. This will send the message to everyone that they can feel safe in taking risks and proposing new ways of doing things. — concludes Leonardo.

— I understand, Leonardo. I think your idea is very good. Let's do it the way you proposed. Miss Stella will formally send the observed non-conformities so that the necessary conversations can take place in your department. What I plan to do, as General Director, is to visit your department, tomorrow morning, to visit the Playful and Interactive Space and observe Filomena in her space. After all, it is something new, and I should get to know it, right? — concludes Teressa.

— Yes, Teressa, certainly! It will be a pleasure to welcome you there. Go whenever you can. And about the Playful and Interactive Space, it is actually Filomena's Workstation, as she now officially becomes our coworker! — celebrates Leonardo.

↑

— Hey, Leonardo... hey...

— What is it, Filomena?

— Since I will be your coworker, in addition to your pet, will I be able to have a companion with me? After all, I don't want to hibernate ahead of time.

— Yes, Filomena. This is in my plans. You can rest assured!

↓

Epilogue

In this work I tried to demonstrate the elements I considered essential to the conception of what happiness is and how it derives from the safety that's transmitted to employees in the workplace in relation to their initiatives. I focused on situations that bother most professionals with difficulty in perceiving their own identity in the face of what they experience in their daily lives.

Whenever there is a lack of definition of what really calls us to enjoy our work, of what gives us real pleasure in carrying out and fulfills us as productive human beings, it is possible that a feeling of helplessness and insecurity occur. There is nothing wrong with this.

When you read this work carefully, you will notice that between one situation and another, the characters are in search of their own truths. This is due to the search of each one for perspectives that will help them determine their effective vocation.

Although, perhaps, a professional has not yet found their real vocation, as this may take much longer for some people than for others, nothing prevents them from seeking happiness in what they are doing at that moment.

Another point I bring is that it is not smart to look only after your heroes, heroines or idols to define your professional career. You need to look inside yourself, trying to get to know yourself better and discuss your professional desires with the people you care for and for whom you have equal affection and admiration.

What is at stake in this search journey is your unconditional happiness. Don't make the mistake of confusing your success with the success of other people. Your success is intimate, personal, non-transferable and has meaning to you primarily, and the more this is correct and makes you very happy, the more other people will see that you got there.

Do not be afraid to be happy. There is no wrong or right profession, bigger or smaller, better or worse. What there are, are professions performed by people who have found their human reason to exist in it and that is why they are happy, or professions performed by people who are still in search of their own human essence. The beauty of it all is that you will never be sure which group you are in until you put yourself to the test.

A big hug and thank you for dedicating some of your time to this book. I hope it was worth it, it was fruitful and meaningful. Look for your happiness and you will find your success! Be happy!

↑

— Shhh ... Leonardo! Tell them there's the post-epilogue coming, okay?

↓

Marcus Garcia de Almeida, Oct-2020
#DoYouThinkImStupid?

Post-epilogue

On the balcony of the company building, there is a large glass area that offers a privileged view. Nature and city mix and are bathed by the sun that, at this hour, heads towards the sunset, around 4:30 pm on that Monday, December 16, 2019.

Leonardo is contemplative, admiring this wonderfully romantic vision. He has arrived early and is waiting for the rest of the Board meeting to begin, which will take place shortly in the main hall, next to the balcony.

Directors, officers and colleagues from top management come and go slowly. They are walking peacefully, as people who are resolved and satisfied with their lives. They watch Leonardo through the wide glass, who is looking out at the balcony. With his hand in the right pocket of his jacket... contemplative!

They do not interrupt him... they just look at him sideways... in their minds and universes of feelings.

A discreet chatter buzz is taking shape inside the hall, while people take their seats waiting for the meeting time.

He was summoned by the company's President, Joanna, to speak at the opening of the Board meeting and explain about the newest initiative in the

Marketing and Products department, strategically envisioned by the General Director, Teressa and fully supported by the Presidency.

The Board should decide on a set of immediate actions to implement strategies that adhere to the context of increasing employee happiness in all departments.

Attentive to the landscape, someone calls him ...

↑

— Hey, Leonardo... hey...

— What is it?

— Did you hear what the managers and some directors are saying?

— Yes, I heard ... why?

— Do you think that the movement and visits to your department will be very large in the coming days because of this?

— It is likely that we will have visits, but not in large quantities.

— And do you think they will make other spaces similar to mine?

— What should probably happen is some fellow managers and even directors being asked by their employees about what they are going to do to transform their own departments, but I don't think they will do anything as unusual as I did.

— And you think this is good?

— Yes, I think so, because before they did nothing, now at least they will try to do something to modify, transform, shake things up, anyway...

— And what do you plan to do?

— Keep challenging...

↓

***

www.idearios.com.br

***

Also available in podcast.

Digital editing and cover: IDEÁRIO

Curitiba, PR

© 2020 by Profissionais.com

About the author:

Marcus Garcia de Almeida

Educator, Specialist in Knowledge Management, Specialist in Emotional Intelligence, Master in Science, Management and Information Technology.

Lecturer and professor, active in the studies of Management, Education, Teacher Training, Communication, Strategic Sustainability, Corporate Governance, Logical Thinking, Decision-Making Process, Learning for Children and Adults, Applied Technologies and Strategy.

Director of IDEÁRIO, publishing house about Theory of Knowledge (epistemology), Causality and the Human Being.

Researcher in education, management, communication and innovation.

Author of hundreds of publications among books, manuals, scientific articles, chronicles and essays. Active in university teaching for graduate and post-graduate courses in several Brazilian institutions. Mentor.

@professormarcusgarcia

About this book:

Format	5,5" x 8,5"
Graphic Spot	4,8" x 8"
Typology used	Futura Md BT (Cover)
	Yrsa 12 pt (Text)
	Futura MdCn BT (Titles)
	Calibri Light (Ned notes)
Paper	Cream 80gsm
Cover	Bright

End notes

[1] **careerists** - A person whose main concern is for professional advancement, especially one willing to achieve this by any means.

[2] **gossipers** - A person who habitually spreads intimate or private rumors or facts.

[3] **visceral** - Being or arising from impulse or sudden emotion rather than from thought or deliberation.

[4] **SUV** - According to the Merriam-Webster dictionary, a "sport utility vehicle" is "a rugged automotive vehicle like a station wagon but built on a light-truck chassis". The "SUV" term is defined as "a large vehicle that is designed to be used on rough surfaces but that is often used on city roads or highways." The "SUV" acronym "is still used to describe nearly anything with available all-wheel drive and raised ground clearance."

[5] **latent anxiety** - Although currently classified as a somatoform disorder, cognitive-behavioral models conceptualize hypochondriasis (HC) as a severe form of health anxiety. The Short Health Anxiety Inventory (SHAI) is a measure derived from this conceptualization that measures health anxiety symptoms across the range of severity.

[6] **throw in the towel** - A boxer's seconds throw a towel into the ring to signal that they want to stop the fight and save him further punishment.

[7] **innovative spirit** - An innovative spirit is a mindset that actively seeks change rather than waiting to adapt to change. In other words, it's a super-positive mindset that embraces critical questioning, creative and continuous improvement. It's about taking ownership and pride in your organization.

[8] **to break the routine** - Sometimes, you simply can't take it anymore. The level of boredom has reached a point where you start appreciating that guy's awful jokes at the office, and perhaps even the bills coming in your mailbox – anything to break the monotony.

[9] **highly efficient and effective gears** - This is something that each business will need if they want to have a high level of business potential energy. Your business is doing things that increase business potential energy, and that things are done in a right way. So, the business potential energy is converted into kinetic energy. These types of activities will give you the results that will increase your profitability. For example, this is the case when you choose the right products that you sell in a right way. In such a way, you will assure a long-term success of you as an entrepreneur and your business at the same time.

[10] **human nature** - The general psychological characteristics, feelings, and behavioral traits of humankind, regarded as shared by all humans.

[11] **stagnant** - Not flowing or moving, and often foul-smelling or stale: stagnant ponds; stagnant air. "i.e. I am the same person I was last year." 15 years ago, I realized that statement was a dubious accomplishment. Twelve months had gone by, and I had little to show for it. I hadn't moved forward. I was stagnant. The definition of stagnant is someone or something that has little or no movement or activity.

[12] **cycle of continuous improvement** - Continuous improvement is an ongoing effort to improve products, services or processes. These efforts can seek "incremental" improvement over time or "breakthrough" improvement all at once. Among the most widely used tools for continuous improvement is a four-step quality model—the plan-do-check-act (PDCA) cycle, also known as Deming Cycle or Shewhart Cycle: Plan: Identify an opportunity and plan for change. Do: Implement the change on a small scale. Check: Use data to analyze the results of the change and determine whether it made a difference. Act: If the change was successful, implement it on a wider scale and continuously assess your results. If the change did not work, begin the cycle again.

[13] **process improvement** - A continual improvement process, also often called a continuous improvement process (abbreviated as CIP or CI), is an ongoing effort to improve products, services, or processes. These efforts can seek "incremental" improvement over time or "breakthrough" improvement all at once. Delivery (customer valued) processes are constantly evaluated and improved in the light of their efficiency, effectiveness and flexibility.

[14] **essentially utilitarian questions** - Utilitarianism is a family of normative ethical theories that prescribe actions that maximize happiness and well-being for all affected individuals. Although different varieties of utilitarianism admit different characterizations, the basic idea behind all of them is to in some sense maximize utility, which is often defined in terms of well-being or related concepts. For instance, Jeremy Bentham, the founder of utilitarianism, described utility as "that property in any object, whereby it tends to produce benefit, advantage, pleasure, good, or happiness...[or] to prevent the happening of mischief, pain, evil, or unhappiness to the party whose interest is considered."

[15] **egotistical** - Concerned chiefly or only with yourself and your advantage to the exclusion of others; e.g. "Selfish men were...trying to make capital for themselves out of the sacred cause of civil rights"- Maria Weston Chapman.

[16] **holistically** - "The whole is greater than the sum of its parts" expresses the essence of holism, a term coined by the great South African general and statesman Jan Smuts in 1926. Holism generally opposes the Western tendency toward analysis, the breaking down of wholes into parts sometimes to the point that "you can't see the forest for the trees". Holism is an important concept in the sciences and social sciences.

[17] **startupper** - An entrepreneur who is a founder/co-founder of a startup.

[18] **ostentatious** - characterized by pretentious, showy, or vulgar display.

[19] **strategic tactical level** - The tactical plan describes the tactics the organization plans to use to achieve the ambitions outlined in the strategic plan. It is a short range (i.e. with a scope of less than one year), low-level document that breaks down the broader mission statements into smaller, actionable chunks. If the strategic plan is a response to "What?", the tactical plan responds to "How?". Creating tactical plans is usually handled by mid-level managers. The tactical plan is a very flexible document; it can hold anything, and everything required to achieve the organization's goals. That said, there are some components shared by most tactical plans: 1. Specific Goals with Fixed Deadlines: Suppose your organization's aim is to become the largest shoe retailer in the city. The tactical plan will break down this broad ambition into smaller, actionable goals. The goal(s) should be highly specific and have fixed deadlines to spur action — expand to two stores within three months, grow at 25% per quarter, or increase revenues to $1mn within six months, and so on. 2. Budgets: The tactical plan should list budgetary requirements to achieve the aims specified in the strategic plan. This should include the budget for hiring personnel, marketing, sourcing, manufacturing, and running the day-to-day operations of the company. Listing the revenue outflow/inflow is also a recommended practice. 3. Resources: The tactical plan should list all the resources you can muster to achieve the organization's aims. This should include human resources, IP, cash resources, etc. Again, being highly specific is encouraged. (From UDEMY Blog, by Udemy Editor).

[20] **leap of faith** - An act of believing something that is not easily believed.

[21] **dantesque** - Of, pertaining to, or in the style of Dante; characterized by a formal, elevated tone and somber focus.

[22] **Goethe** - German writer and scientist. A master of poetry, drama, and the novel, he spent 50 years on his two-part dramatic poem Faust (published 1808 and 1832). He also conducted scientific research in various fields, notably botany, and held several governmental positions.

[23] **alter ego** - 1. a second self. 2. a very close and intimate friend.

[24] **stimulus responses** - The model allows the prediction of a quantitative response to a quantitative stimulus, for example one administered by a researcher. ... In psychology, stimulus response theory concerns forms of classical conditioning in which a stimulus becomes paired response in a subject's mind.

[25] **phagocytize** - 1. A process of a cell actively engulfing other cells or food particles. 2. A process by which certain cells engulf and destroy foreign particles or microorganisms such as bacteria.

[26] **scaffold** - A platform used in the execution of condemned prisoners, as by hanging or beheading.

[27] **benefit of the doubt** - The withholding of judgment so as to retain a favorable or at least neutral opinion of someone or something when the full information about the subject is not yet available. e.g. "You're my sister! Can't you give me the benefit of the doubt, instead of believing the worst about me?"; "Let's give him the benefit of the doubt before we start accusing him. There may be a good explanation."

www.ingramcontent.com/pod-product-compliance
Lightning Source LLC
LaVergne TN
LVHW091455170726
843492LV00001B/188